D0849374

DATE DUE

12-18-78			
9-19-79			
2-4-80			
3-8-83			
2/9/83			
9-21-63			
2-7-84			
5-5-92			

BLACK HOLES, WHITE DWARFS, AND SUPERSTARS

EXPLORING OUR UNIVERSE

Illustrated by

Helmut K. Wimmer

BLACK HOLES, WHITE DWARFS, AND SUPERSTARS

FRANKLYN M. BRANLEY

Thomas Y. Crowell Company   New York

Library of Congress Cataloging in Publication Data
Branley, Franklyn Mansfield, 1915–
Black holes, white dwarfs, and superstars.
Bibliography: p. Includes index.
SUMMARY: Using the sun for comparison, examines what
astronomers have learned about pulsars, supergiants,
white dwarfs, and black holes.
1. Stars—Juv. lit. [1. Stars]
I. Wimmer, Helmut K. II. Title.
QB801.7.B69 1976 523 75-42417
ISBN 0-690-01068-0
1 2 3 4 5 6 7 8 9 10

For Peg

by the Author

Exploring Our Universe

Dimensions in this book are given according to the International System of Units (Système Internationale—SI), or metric system, which uses:

meters (*metres*) for length
grams for mass (weight at sea level)
liters (*litres*) for volume

To convert U.S. customary measurements to metric, or metric to customary:

1 inch = 2.54 centimeters	1 centimeter = 0.3937 inch
1 foot = 0.305 meter	1 meter = 39.37 inches
1 yard = 0.914 meter	1 kilometer = 0.621 mile
1 mile = 1.609 kilometers	1 gram = 0.035 ounce
1 pound = 0.454 kilogram	1 kilogram = 2.20 pounds
1 quart = 0.946 liter	1 liter = 1.06 quarts

Acknowledgments

I wish to thank Dr. Catharine D. Garmany for reading this book in manuscript and for making many helpful suggestions. Should inconsistencies remain, they are my responsibility alone. I am also grateful to the Hale Observatories and to the Cerro Tololo Observatory for the photographs they have permitted us to reproduce.

The illustrations by Helmut K. Wimmer listed below according to their page numbers in BLACK HOLES, WHITE DWARFS, AND SUPERSTARS *appeared originally in the following books and magazines. These illustrations are used by the courtesy of the author, illustrator, and publisher.*

Astronomy. *Franklyn M. Branley, Mark R. Chartrand III. Thomas Y. Crowell, 1975. Illustrations copyright © 1975 by Helmut K. Wimmer. Pages 2–3, 8, 10–11, 13, 16 (top), 17, 18, 19, 24, 47, 48, 56–57, 61, 70, 80, 81, 97.*

The Sun: Star Number One. *Franklyn M. Branley. Thomas Y. Crowell, 1964. Illustrations copyright © 1964 by Helmut K. Wimmer. Pages 5, 16 (bottom), 25, 33.*

Scientific American. *Adapted with permission from "Gravitational Collapse," Kip S. Thorne. Copyright © 1967 by Scientific American, Inc. All rights reserved. Page 91.*

Contents

BLACK HOLES,
WHITE DWARFS,
AND SUPERSTARS

FAMILIES OF STARS

The universe is made of stars. In our own galaxy there are at least 100 billion of them, and our galaxy is only medium-sized. There are galaxies that contain 200 billion stars, and even more. And the number of galaxies in the universe is countless. In the area of space which astronomers can observe, there are perhaps 10 billion galaxies. There are billions more that they know about only theoretically.

Our knowledge of the stars is new; the abundance of them, and their nature, only began to be revealed with the development of the telescope in the early 1600s. Understanding of the stars did not advance rapidly until this century, and it is still far from complete. In fact, astronomers agree there is much more about the stars that we don't know than what we do know. Almost as soon as astronomers began to learn what the "average" star is like, they found that there are many stars that differ widely from the average. There are stars that devour matter and light, causing them to disappear forever; stars whose substance is packed as densely as the world's population would be if all the people were enclosed in the head of a pin; stars that wink on and off thirty times a second; stars that are much smaller than the Earth, and others a thousand times bigger than the Sun. Such stars

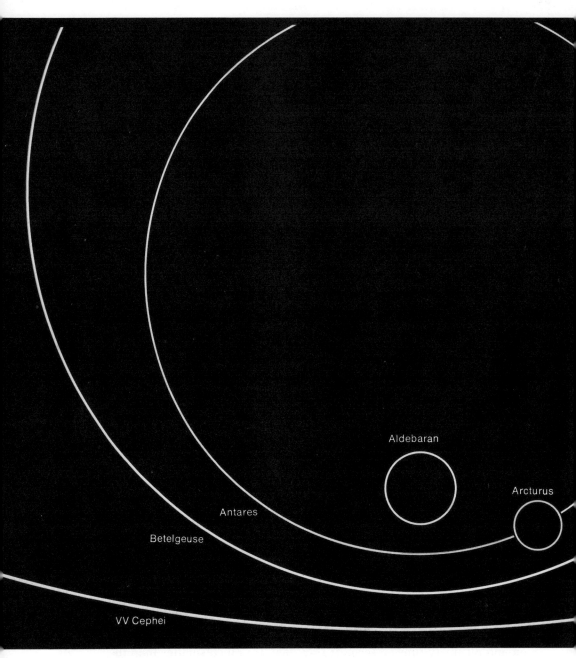

Aldebaran

Arcturus

Antares

Betelgeuse

VV Cephei

Relative sizes of the Earth and Sun, and of the Sun and other stars. At the upper right a neutron star is shown relative to the Earth. If the Earth were reduced to the small dot, then the Sun would be as shown. If the Sun were then reduced to the small dot, Sirius, Vega, Capella, Arcturus and Aldebaran would be about as shown. The solar system out to some 50 million

kilometers beyond Mars could be contained inside the giant star Aldebaran —a diameter of some 560 million kilometers.

The supergiants—Antares, Betelgeuse, VV Cephei—in turn dwarf the giants. The diameter of VV Cephei is so great that the entire solar system, some 12 000 million kilometers across, could be contained inside it.

are truly incredible. They are exotic stars—strange, unusual, extraordinary.

Astronomers have observed many of these stars, and they find it hard to believe what their telescopes reveal. There are probably more mysteries about such superstars than there are solid facts. In this book we'll explore what astronomers have learned about pulsars, supergiants, white dwarfs, black holes. We'll also read about some of their unanswered questions. A look at an ordinary star will help us understand the discoveries astronomers have made about the glamorous stars.

THE SUN—AN ORDINARY STAR

Although it provides us with the energy that keeps us alive, and so is of the greatest importance to us, the Sun is not impressive among the other stars. It is a quite ordinary, average star. There are stars smaller than the Sun, dimmer and cooler and there are stars much larger than the Sun, brighter, hotter—much more energetic in every way. But the Sun is the star nearest to us; it is the one star, among the billions that exist, that we see as a disk. All other stars are so far away that they appear as points of light. Techniques involving electronic intensifying of light and computer reconstruction of images are now making it possible for astronomers to see other stars as disks. However, the Sun remains the only star surface they can study effectively. Because we can see the disk of the Sun clearly, we can study this star closely. By learning about the Sun, we learn about the other stars.

The Sun is about 1 392 000 kilometers in diameter, almost a million miles (864,000)—large enough to contain a million Earths. The material it is made of, mostly hydrogen and helium, is packed together very tightly at the center but loosely at the surface. The mean density of the Sun is 1.41, while that of the Earth is 5.5. The amount of material in the Sun is some 333,000 times more than all the matter contained in the Earth.

The sun is a nuclear furnace. Like the other stars, it gets its energy from the nuclei of atoms. Four protons (the nucleus of a hydrogen atom is a proton) combine to make a single helium nucleus. During the process energy is released, mostly in the form of heat and light.

The Sun is a hydrogen-burning star: one in which protons fuse to produce helium plus vast amounts of energy. In the process four protons (the nuclei of hydrogen atoms) combine to produce helium 4. Along the way deuterium (hydrogen 2), gamma radiation, neutrinos, and helium 3 are also produced.

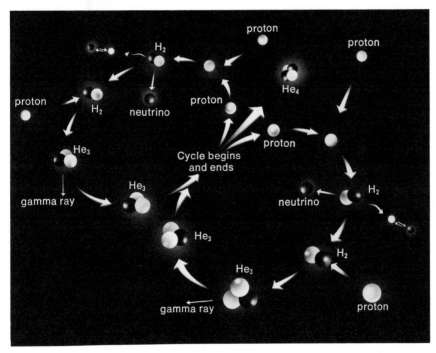

Some of the mass of the Sun thus is converted into energy. Every second about 500 million tons of hydrogen become helium, and another 4 million tons go out of existence—they become energy. A quantity of 4 million tons is a tremendous mass. (Mass is the amount of material. Density indicates whether the material is spread out thinly or packed together tightly.) The Sun contains so much material that it could continue shining with the same brightness for billions of years, and probably will.

The process by which hydrogen becomes helium is fusion. The Sun is a nuclear fusion reactor. So are the other stars. The process in other stars may vary from that in the Sun, but their source of energy is still fusion in some form.

The idea of fusion was first proposed by Albert Einstein in the early years of this century. But not until the 1930s was the principle used to explain the vast energy produced in stellar furnaces. For centuries, ever since it was realized that stars are gaseous formations, people had been perplexed by the need to explain the source of the Sun's energy. Many theories were offered.

Since on the Earth heat is associated with fire, it was suggested that the Sun is on fire. Champions of this idea pointed out that the Sun is made of gases that burn, hydrogen for instance. As the hydrogen burned (combined with oxygen), heat was produced, they said. This idea is not unreasonable, except that when one figured out the amount of fuel needed to produce the energy of the Sun by burning, it was apparent that the supply would last a very short time—not more than two or three thousand years.

Another suggestion was that the Sun is contracting, and that as the material in the Sun packs together heat is generated. The idea was sound, because heat is generated as gravity pulls material closer to the center of a spherical body. If the Sun contracted 60 meters in a year, that would be sufficient to produce its energy. Such a small contraction would not even be noticed from the Earth until millions of years had passed. This theory was widely accepted a century ago because it accounted for the production of solar energy over a long period. At that time scientists did not know that the Earth is much older than a few million years—actually billions of years old; nor did they know that the Sun had been shining for billions of years. However, until geological studies revealed the age of the Earth, the contraction explanation for the heat of the Sun was quite adequate.

THE STARS AND EARLY MAN

Our knowledge of the energy of the stars is new. Actually most of our general information about the stars is recent. Two thousand years ago men believed that the stars were all contained in a great sphere. According to some of the ancient Greeks, the Earth was at the center of everything. The Sun, Moon, and each of the then known planets (Mercury, Venus, Mars, Jupiter, and Saturn) were fastened to turning spheres that surrounded the Earth. The spheres were like transparent shells or layers around the Earth. The outermost shell, it was said, was the sphere of the stars—the boundary of the universe. The innermost sphere was the region of the Moon. The planets were on spheres located between these two extremes.

The nature of the stars was explained in many different ways. According to some of the ancients, stars were lanterns of the gods, hung in the sky. Another idea held that the stars were holes in the outermost sphere. Beyond the sphere was everlasting brightness, and wherever there was a hole that brightness shone through.

The ancient Egyptians believed the universe to be their country, surrounded by high mountains. The Sun was carried in a boat that at night moved behind a mountain peak. The stars were lamps hung from the sky.

Stars were important in the mythology of the ancients, for they imagined that various groups of stars (the constellations) were the abodes of their heroes and other characters in their legends. But stars were important for navigation too. Long before they knew the nature of the stars, early men recognized that stars could be used as guides. Early astronomers compiled catalogues of stars, listed them (by name usually), and gave their positions at various seasons.

Before the early seventeenth century, when telescopes were developed, astronomers were concerned with objects that could be observed with the unaided eye: the brighter stars (those used for navigation), the planets, and the Moon. The telescope changed things; for example, it revealed that the stars were thousands of times more numerous than anyone had dreamed. However, people persisted in the belief that all stars were the same distance from the Earth, located on a star sphere. This idea was not changed until the nineteenth century, when distances to stars began to be measured and men discovered that the stars are very far away, at distances that are astounding.

Not until the twentieth century did the nature of stars become known: what they are made of, how they get their energy, how they came into existence, their life histories from birth to death.

EARLY HISTORY OF THE SUN

The most widely accepted explanation of the origin of the universe is the "Big Bang" theory. It holds that some 20 billion years ago (a billion is a thousand million, and man has existed for only 4 million years at most), the matter of the universe was concentrated in one mass. There was a great explosion and, in moments, the elements of the early universe were created. These were mainly hydrogen and

As presently understood, the universe is as shown at the cross point, pages 10 and 11. Several theories attempt to explain where it came from, and what its future will be.

The steady-state theory maintains that the average density of the universe remains the same for all time. The pulsating theory proposes that the universe expands, then contracts, only to expand again. The "Big Bang" theory holds that the universe began in a supercolossal explosion of a primeval "atom." All the stars and galaxies were formed from material once contained in that atom; expansion will continue forever.

Steady-state
universe

Pulsating universe

Universe at present

"Big Bang" universe

H.K.W.

helium. Heavier elements were also produced, but all of these to-gether made up only a small part of the total. Today, 99 percent of the universe is still hydrogen.

Some of the matter in the early universe condensed and formed stars. Those stars that contained massive amounts of material lasted only a few million years. They burned brightly and exploded, blow-ing off their outer layers. As they did, heavy elements were produced.

Remnants of these early stars became gas and dust clouds. (In astronomy, "gas" usually means hydrogen and helium; heavier ele-ments are referred to as "dust.")

A hundred million years or more went by. The cloud which was to become the Sun was several light years in diameter. (A light year is the distance light travels in a year—at its speed of 186,000 miles per second—or some 6,000,000,000,000 miles. In the metric system the speed of light is 3×10^{10} centimeters per second, and a light year is 10^{18} centimeters.) The gas and dust in the cloud churned about. Atoms collided with one another, then went separate ways. There came a time when two or more of these colliding atoms slowed down and held together; a new and larger mass was created. This larger mass had a greater gravitational attraction. Other particles were at-tracted to it, and so it grew. Still larger mass meant still greater gravitation, and this meant still more particles.

Millions of tons of matter—hydrogen and helium from the Big Bang, and heavier elements that came from old exploded stars—packed together. Gravitational energy pulled in the atoms. In the process gravitational energy was converted into heat energy. The mass became hotter and hotter, reaching some 10 million degrees Celsius—hot enough to fuse hydrogen atoms. The mass had become a star, a gaseous formation in which one kind of matter is converted into another, and in which matter is converted into energy. It had become a nuclear fusion furnace.

And so, about 5 billion years ago, the Sun came into existence. After a few explosive events, the gaseous mass settled down. Except for a few rare, short-lived deviations, it has ever since been producing the same amount of energy it now radiates. And it will continue to do so for another 5 billion years or so.

The life of the Sun. It originated essentially from gases produced by the Big Bang (1). The gases packed together and became hotter, and nuclear fusion began (2). After some 8 to 10 billion years the Sun will expand, becoming a cool red giant star (3). After thousands of years of pulsating, the Sun will cool (4); and it may explode (5). Ultimate cooling will cause it to become a small dwarf star (6), perhaps no larger than the Earth.

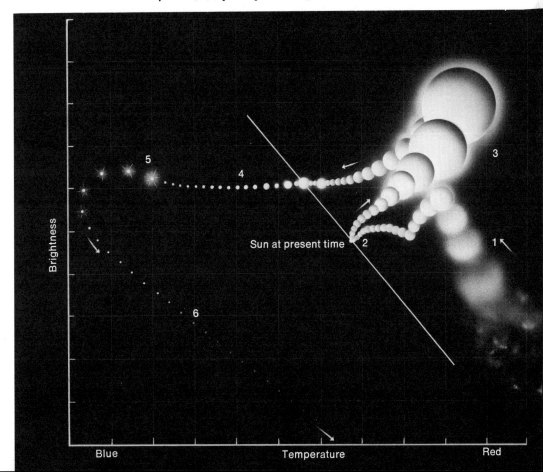

THE FATE OF THE SUN

Eventually the Sun will become much larger than it is now. It will change from a yellow star to a red star. The solar surface will extend into space as far as the Earth, perhaps somewhat farther. Our planet will be inside the Sun.

As time passes, the Sun's hydrogen will become used up. There will not be sufficient hydrogen for the hydrogen-to-helium reaction to continue. Helium will become the basic fuel. It will fuse together to make carbon and heavier elements, and, as before, energy will be set free.

As one fuel is consumed, the fusion process will utilize other elements. But the process cannot continue forever. The end will occur when the fusion reactions produce iron. Fusion reactions involving iron cannot release energy since the reactions require more energy than they give off. The fate of the star is sealed: it must gradually cool down. As the Sun cools, it will become smaller and smaller—shrinking to a body no larger than the Earth.

THE FAMILY OF STARS

If we were to take the temperature of the stars, we'd find that the Sun's temperature at the surface is about 6 000°K. (The "K" refers to the Kelvin scale. In this scale absolute zero—the coldest anything can get—is 0°; the freezing point of water is 273°; its boiling point is 373°.) Cool stars have a temperature of about 3 500°K, and hot stars may have a surface temperature of 60 000°K. The cool stars are red in color, the hot stars white or blue-white. The Sun is a yellow-orange star—in between.

In the early part of this century Ejnar Hertzsprung, a Danish astronomer, and Henry Norris Russell, an American, plotted nearby stars on a graph. The color (or temperature) of the star was given along the horizontal part of the graph, called the abscissa. Red, cool stars were at the right. Stars with higher temperatures were placed farther to the left.

Hertzsprung and Russell also measured the brightness of the stars. They plotted brightness, or luminosity, along the vertical part of the graph, called the ordinate. The dimmest stars were at the bottom, and the brightest at the top.

When this was done for scores of nearby stars, the astronomers found that the stars were concentrated in some areas of the graph. Other areas contained no stars at all, or only a few. When bright but more distant stars were included, it was seen that most stars fell in a pattern that made a smooth S-curve from the upper left to the lower right. Since most stars were located here, the region was called the main sequence. The arrangement is known as the Hertzsprung-Russell diagram, or simply the H-R diagram. It is of immense value to astronomers because it shows quickly how stars are related and also provides a framework for understanding how the stars began, their life cycles, and how they end.

Notice the position of the Sun (page 16). It is about halfway between red and blue, and also about halfway between the dim and bright extremes. The Sun is an ordinary, or medium, star. Red stars, at the far right, turn out to be dim stars; blue stars, on the far left, turn out to be very bright stars. But there are exceptions. Occasionally we find a red star that is very bright. To be so bright, that star must be very large. It is called a red giant. If it is extremely bright, the star is called a supergiant. Notice where they are located on the diagram.

Astronomers occasionally find stars that are blueish in color but

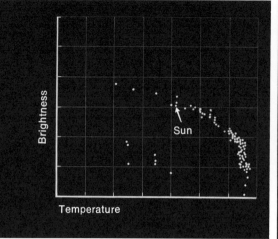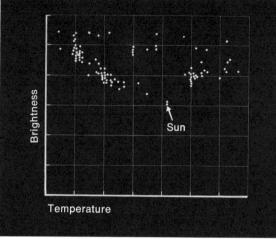

When the temperature and brightness of the stars nearest the Sun are compared (left), it is seen that most are cooler than the Sun, and dimmer.

A diagram of stars that appear brighter than the Sun is shown at the right.

When the near stars, the bright stars, and others in the solar neighborhood are plotted, the main sequence emerges. Giant stars and white dwarf stars are exceptions from the majority.

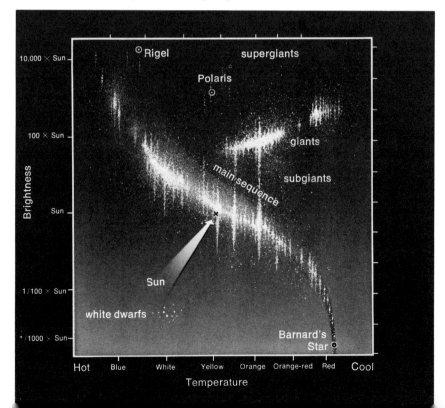

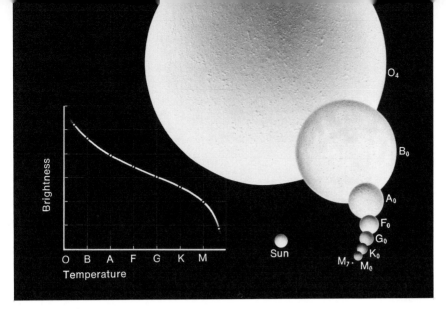

O and B type stars are large, massive, very hot, and short-lived. K and M type stars are small, less massive than the Sun, cool, and long-lived. The Sun is a medium star.

dim. Blue stars should be bright. If one is not, then the star must be very small. It is called a dwarf star, or white dwarf. Notice where they are placed on the diagram. Also notice that there are not many of them. Dwarf stars and giants are among the extraordinary stars.

MAIN SEQUENCE OF STARS

When the mass of material that was to become the Sun began to glow, the mass was 10,000 times its present size; it reached as far as the present orbit of Pluto. In a very short time—perhaps no more than 20 years—the mass collapsed so much that its outer limit would have been the region of Mercury. For the next 50 million years or so the mass continued to grow smaller. As it contracted, temperature increased. The interior of the Sun is now probably about 14 million degrees K.

Nuclear reactions, such as fusion, produce not only energy but outward pressure. The push outward balances the pull of gravity inward; the mass does not grow larger and it does not grow any smaller. The Sun is in equilibrium, and it is converting hydrogen to helium. It is in the main sequence of the H-R diagram.

Suppose the original cloud of material that was to become the Sun had been more massive (contained more material). What would have happened?

If a mass were two times the solar mass (often written $M_\odot$ —the symbol $\odot$ representing the Sun), the star formed would be hotter than the Sun and brighter. If the mass equaled $4M_\odot$, the star would still fall in the main sequence but it would be extremely bright and very hot.

If there were less material than $1M_\odot$, the resulting star would be smaller than the Sun, and cooler. Should the original mass be about

When stars having a mass greater than the Sun reach the main sequence, they "burn" bright and fast. Those having less mass than the Sun reach the main sequence far to the right; they "burn" dimly but for a long, long time.

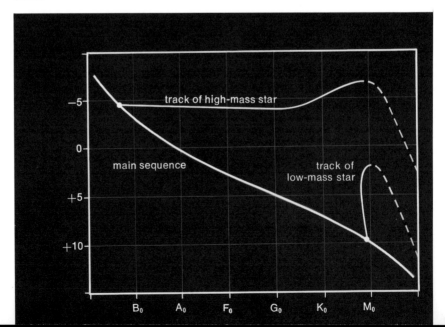

0.08M$_\odot$, the resulting star would equal the smallest of known red stars. When the mass is as small as about 0.05M$_\odot$ (5 percent of the solar mass), the material never reaches the main sequence. The mass simply cools down and ends as a black dwarf.

Main-sequence stars have masses that range from about four times the mass of the Sun to about eight hundredths of it. This does not mean there are not more massive stars. In fact, the most massive stars observed up till now may be fifty times the solar mass. There may be stars that contain 100M$_\odot$ —but if they exist at all they must last a very short time. Indeed, there may be supermassive objects that contain a million solar masses.

GRAVITATION

Gravitation is an ever-present force in the universe. It is the force

In a star that is in equilibrium, pressures on any given volume must balance out, as shown at the right. Otherwise the star would expand or collapse. At the left is represented the temperature flow in such a star. Energy out of a given volume (a cube, for example) must equal the difference between energy in and whatever energy may be produced in the volume itself.

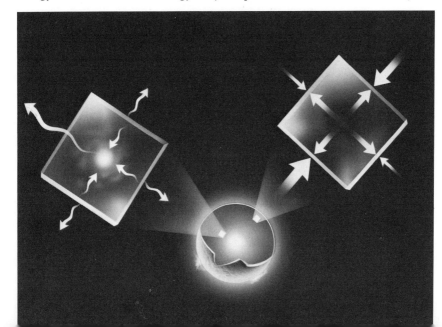

that pulled gases together and made the Sun and the other stars. It is the force that raised interior temperature high enough to start nuclear reactions. Gravitation is the force that holds the Sun together, keeping the pressure of heat from blowing it apart.

The persistence of gravitation will ultimately collapse our Sun into a dwarf star. It will collapse more massive stars and cause them to explode. It will shatter atoms, pack neutrons together so a thimbleful would weigh a million tons, compress matter so the mass is infinite. Gravitation will pull matter together and pack it into a black hole where it will disappear, and from which it may emerge eventually in another universe, or reappear in ours as an explosive quasar.

Strange?

It certainly is. Pulsars, variable stars, giants and supergiants, white dwarfs, black holes—these and other kinds of exotic stars all result from the force of gravitation pulling a star together, and the force of thermal pressure pushing a star apart.

Now that we have some idea of what an ordinary star is, where it came from, why it is ordinary and has a place in the main sequence of the H-R diagram, let's look at the superstars.

YOUNG STARS

T TAURI STARS

You recall that the Sun is a main-sequence star. This means it is converting hydrogen into helium, and the resulting pressure pushing outward is balanced by the gravitation pulling inward; the star is in equilibrium. Stars of less than one solar mass that have not quite reached the main sequence, those that have not reached equilibrium, are called T Tauri stars.

About a thousand of them have been studied. The name comes from the first of this type of star that was observed. A capital letter before a star name means that the star is variable—its brightness changes. Sometimes the changes occur at regular intervals, in cycles that vary from a few hours to a few days, weeks, or years. In T Tauri stars the changes are irregular.

Before there were powerful telescopes, astronomers decided to refer to variable stars in a constellation by using capital letters beginning with R and going to Z. The letter was placed in front of the possessive form of the Latin name for the constellation. For example, the first variable star that was discovered in the constellation Taurus is called R Tauri. (T Tauri was the third one.) As larger telescopes were invented, more variable stars were found. This meant the system

of lettering had to be expanded. Double letters were used: so there would be RR Tauri, RS, RT, and through to RZ; then SS, ST, and so on; and continuing until ZZ. But even more variables than could be identified using this system were found in some constellations. The method was expanded by including AA, AB, AC, and continuing to AZ; BB to BZ; and so on. This notation allows for 334 variable stars in a given constellation. When there are more than 334 they are referred to by number, beginning with 335, preceded by V—as V335 Tauri, for example.

T Tauri stars were first studied and named in the 1940s by Alfred H. Joy, an astronomer who was then at Mount Palomar Observatory. Every T Tauri star that he found was embedded in dust clouds, and bright massive blue-white stars were always close by.

It was known that hot massive stars are young. They have to be. Because of very high temperatures and pressures, they use up hydrogen a million times faster than the Sun. At such a rate, huge hot stars can last only a few million years at most—in many cases much less. While this is a long time when compared with man's existence, it is very short in terms of ages of less massive stars. For example, the lifetime of the Sun is probably 10,000 million years. Since T Tauri stars and short-lived giant stars are found together, both are probably of a similar age. There were other reasons as well for believing T Tauris were young stars. One was the bright-line spectrum.

Astronomers study light with a spectroscope, an instrument that separates light into the various wavelengths of which it is made. Light enters the spectroscope through a narrow slit and strikes a prism (or diffraction grating); the viewer sees the different wavelengths as colored lines ranging from red through orange, yellow, green, blue, and violet. If a hot, densely packed gas such as is found inside the

T Tauri stars are found in gaseous clouds that are associated with young, highly active blue-white stars.

The location in Orion of this bright nebula is indicated in the inset. (Hale Observatories)

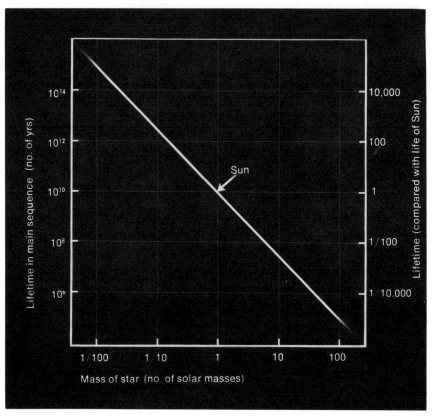

Stars less massive than the Sun (to the left) last thousands of times longer than do Sun-type stars. The more massive the star (toward the right), the shorter its lifetime—only a fraction of that of the Sun.

Sun or another star were observed, separate lines would not be seen. Instead one would see wide bands of color, each blending into the next. This is because the Sun's light energy originates deep inside it, where the gases are packed together tightly. Each atom there produces its own energy, with its own characteristic wavelength, which

There are three basic types of spectra.

A hot, dense energy source, such as the filament of a bulb (or the interior of the Sun), produces a continuous spectrum.

A hot, nebulous gas, such as sodium vapor from salt held in a flame (or the atmosphere of the Sun), produces a bright-line spectrum.

When a continuous spectrum passes through a hot gas, the gas removes some energy in those wavelengths it ordinarily produces. The result is a dark-line, or absorption, spectrum.

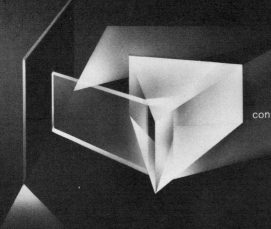

continuous spectrum

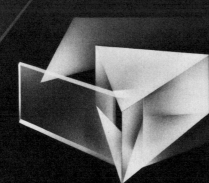

bright-line spectrum

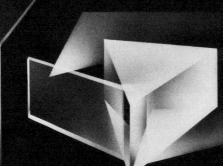

dark-line spectrum

would show up in a spectrogram as a series of bright color lines. However, because the atoms are so close together in the solar interior, the lines of one kind of atom blend into those of another kind. A continuous spectrum is produced.

When the spectrum is made by hot gases of low density, such as those in the solar atmosphere and the atmosphere of most other stars, the bright color lines of a given kind of atom can be seen distinctly. The colors are sharply separated. A bright-line spectrum is produced.

However, when sunlight and most starlight passes through a spectroscope, neither bright lines nor an ordinary continuous spectrum is seen. Instead, dark lines are produced on a continuous background. The dark lines appear at exactly those locations where there would be bright lines if a gas (hydrogen for example) were heated and studied in a laboratory. The interior of the Sun, which is very hot and dense, produces a continuous spectrum. It is composed of multitudes of bright lines all blended together. In emerging from the Sun, the energy passes through a region called the reversing layer, or photosphere. Energy of certain kinds (wavelengths) is absorbed by this layer. When this occurs, dark lines appear on the otherwise continuous spectrum. When one studies the Sun with a spectroscope, he sees thousands of dark lines, each related to a certain kind of atom, displayed on a band of continuous color. This is true at all times— except during an eclipse.

At the onset of a total solar eclipse, just before the Moon completely covers and blots out the Sun, bright lines are seen at the edge of the Sun. They are produced by hot gases in a lower layer of the Sun's atmosphere called the chromosphere. These bright lines are always there, but generally they cannot be seen because of the much brighter solar surface. Just before total eclipse this bright surface is less apparent, making it possible to see the bright lines.

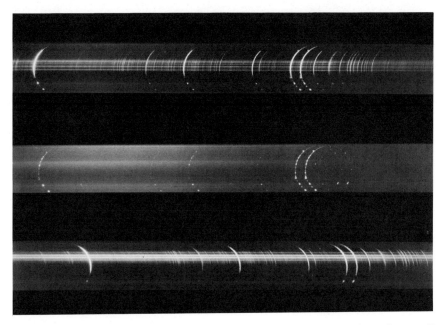

Just before the total phase of a solar eclipse, at the moment of totality, and later just as the Moon begins to reveal the solar surface, a bright-line flash spectrum—produced in the solar chromosphere—can be seen on the spectroscope. (Hale Observatories)

In the Sun the chromosphere is a very shallow layer; it is, however, a region of extreme activity. In young stars the chromosphere is much deeper. The region produces a fantastic amount of energy that shows up as very strong bright lines. The lines are so intense they are stronger than the continuous spectrum produced by the interior of the star. Therefore, when astronomers can associate a bright-line spectrum with a star, they know that the star must be young.

The Sun is an active star. Photographs reveal that great quantities of gas erupt from the surface. In some cases the gases move with enough velocity to resist the pull of gravity, and travel more than a million kilometers from the surface. Solar gravitation overcomes eventually, pulling the gas back in again. In T Tauri stars the activity

The surface of the Sun, here shown in section, is extremely active. However, T Tauri stars are much more energetic—sometimes so violent that parts of them are ejected into space.

is much more energetic. The gases are moving fast enough—up to 300 kilometers a second—to escape the star's gravitation, and are probably lost forever. In 30 million years an early T Tauri probably loses as much material as is contained in the Sun.

By the time a mass of material reaches the stage where it has high chromospheric activity, the star is in an advanced stage of its youth. It began as a mass of cool, dark gas and dust pulled together by gravitation. When the size of the formation was about that of the solar system—some 15 billion kilometers across—it was still cool and dark. The mass continued to contract, but temperature did not rise rapidly because large amounts of the energy were used in breaking hydrogen molecules (H_2) into hydrogen atoms (H) and also in ionizing atoms (removing electrons). Since pressure outward was low, the mass of material collapsed rapidly. In a few months it shrank to some 150 million kilometers across. The collapse then stopped because enough heat built up to exert outward pressure sufficient to equal the inward attraction. The mass became visible as a bright red star.

We know that stars do not last forever, yet the number of stars remains essentially unchanged. New stars are continually being born —at the stupendously rapid rate of one star somewhere in our galaxy every 500 to 1000 years. In 1936 a new star called FU Orionis was discovered; the star appeared in the constellation Orion where there had been none previously. It is entirely possible that other masses of material now collapsing will become stars and will be discovered tomorrow, next month, or next year.

T Tauri stars may take 50 million years to collapse enough to become stable, well-behaved stars. That means temperature at the core will have reached 10 million degrees K, nuclear reactions converting hydrogen to helium will have begun, and energy released during the process sustains outward pressure, preventing further collapse.

The H-R diagram on page 30 shows the location of the Sun in relation to several T Tauri stars. The soft S-curve is the main sequence. Stars of greater mass than the Sun are toward the left, those of less mass toward the right. T Tauri stars are shown by the dots. Notice they are above the main sequence, indicating that they are more luminous (give out more energy) than the Sun. For the most part their surface

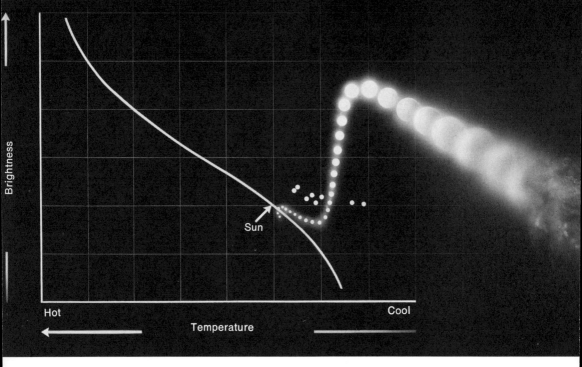

The birth of a T Tauri star, from its formation out of a cloud of gas and dust to its arrival in the main sequence. The other dots show the locations of several such stars on the H-R diagram.

temperatures are a bit lower than that of the Sun—meaning that, since they are brighter, they must be larger than the sun.

The creation of a single T Tauri star is shown here. We do not know how much time was needed for the original gas and dust cloud to become consolidated into a star-making mass (that would be represented far to the right off the page). But once the period of rapid contraction begins, the mass would take only about 20 years to collapse to the size of the solar system, and only a few months more to collapse further to the point of becoming a visible red star—as shown in the movement from right to left and the sharp vertical drop. For some 50 million years temperature remains about the same, though the star continues to contract. Temperature then builds up

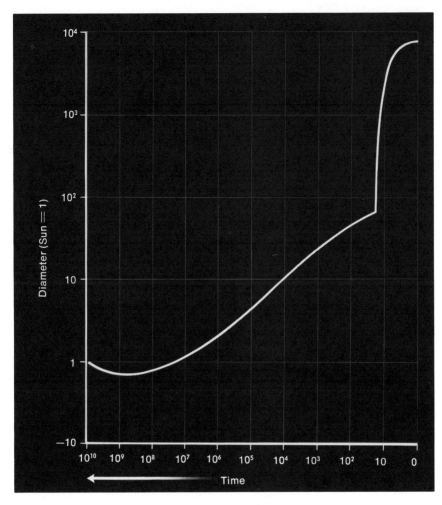

How the Sun may have evolved from the original gas cloud to a hydrogen-burning star.

(as shown by the short right-to-left path) and the star reaches stability; it has entered the main sequence. If its mass is about equal to that of the Sun, the new star will remain in the main sequence for 10 billion years.

A close-up of the stages in the history of a T Tauri star is shown on page 31. This is the story of the Sun, which at one time was a T Tauri star. Diameters are shown vertically, from less than that of the present Sun, at the bottom, to 10,000 times the Sun's diameter (equal to the distance from the Sun out to Pluto), at the top. Time is shown horizontally, from 0 years at the right to 10 billion years at the left. Looking at the far right, we see that the period of rapid collapse took only about 20 years, and most of it was completed in a matter of weeks (the line is straight downward). Further collapse occurred over the next several million years. The mass decreased to the present size of the Sun, at which time nuclear reactions started. There was continued contraction, followed by expansion until once again the size of the present Sun was reached.

ROTATION OF T TAURI STARS

The Sun is so close to us that we can see it as a disk. Occasionally we see irregularities of the surface moving from one side of the Sun to the other. After making several observations, astronomers could conclude that the entire Sun is spinning around. A turn is completed in about 26 days, which is a long rotation period for a star.

Another way of finding the Sun's rotation is by measuring its Doppler shift. In the early part of the last century Christian Johann Doppler (1803–1853), an Austrian scientist, believed that when a light source is moving toward you, its spectral lines are shifted to-

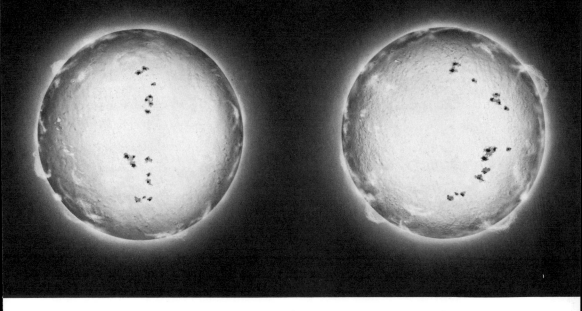

The changing positions of sunspots (here shown stylized) enable deter-mination of the Sun's rotation. It is so slow that it would not be noticeable from the nearest stars.

ward the blue (shorter) wavelengths, and that they shift toward the red (longer) wavelengths when the light source is moving away from the observer. The idea was later proved correct by the French phys-icist Armand Hippolyte Louis Fizeau (1819–1896). The phenomenon is now called the Doppler-Fizeau effect, or simply the Doppler effect.

When light from one edge of the Sun passes through a spectro-scope, the spectral lines show a blue shift (coming toward the ob-server), while light from the opposite edge shows an equivalent red shift (moving away from the observer). The amount of shift is what would be expected when the movement toward and away is about 2 kilometers a second. (Actually, the period of rotation of the Sun, and so its speed, varies with latitude: some 24 days along the solar equator, increasing to 27 days in the polar regions of the Sun.)

The rotation speed of the Sun is so low that it could not be noticed if the Sun were as far away as the nearest star.

All stars except the Sun are so far away that they appear as points of light. There is no way of measuring Doppler shifts of light from their edges, as can be done with the Sun. However, spectrograms of these distant stars provide clues as to their rotation, at least when the rotation is rapid.

Spectral lines are ordinarily sharply defined. When they are broad and fuzzy—spread out somewhat—the reason may be that the point source (the star) is rotating. (Or it could be that the star is giving off large amounts of hot, bright gases.) Among stable stars, those in the main sequence, there is a connection between mass and rotation. The more massive the star, the faster it rotates. Stars that have masses, say, ten times that of the Sun rotate some 200 kilometers a second; those less massive than the Sun rotate at speeds under 2 kilometers a second.

If the fuzzy lines of T Tauri stars result only from rotation, the speed must be very fast—fifty or more times faster than the Sun. Very likely, however, the loss of gases from the star also contributes to the fuzzy appearance.

Variability in the brightness of T Tauris may also result from rotation. Their variations may occur within only a few hours, or within a few days or a month. It is believed that these cyclic variations are possibly the result of the star's rotation: active areas are turned toward us, then carried to the far side of the sky, to be seen again during the next half turn. Conclusions about periods of rotation arrived at from observations of variations agree very closely with conclusions reached by observing fuzziness of the spectral lines. It seems safe to say that T Tauris rotate rapidly.

LITHIUM IN T TAURI STARS

Stars are the most abundant formations in the universe, and the main ingredient of the universe is hydrogen. It follows, then, that the most common substance in stars is hydrogen. Many stars contain nothing but hydrogen and helium. Other stars, such as the Sun, contain small percentages of other elements—boron, krypton, oxygen, iron, carbon. Stars that contain materials in addition to hydrogen and helium are called metallic stars.

T Tauri stars are essentially hydrogen, but they also contain traces of other materials. We could expect this, for T Tauris always occur in dust clouds. (In astronomy, you recall, "dust" means all substances other than hydrogen and helium.) A curious condition of these stars is the abundance of lithium—several hundred times more than the percentage in the Sun. The Sun was at some time a T Tauri star. What has happened to the lithium it once contained? This is just one of the questions about the nature of T Tauri stars that perplex astronomers. However, answers to it have been suggested.

Stony meteorites found on the Earth strengthen the belief that the Sun used to contain a lot more lithium than it does at present. Meteorites are probably bits of material left over when the Sun was created. They are pieces of the cloud from which the Sun was formed that somehow never became consolidated into the Sun. Analysis of the meteorites reveals that lithium is thirty-five times more abundant in them than it is in the present-day Sun.

It is believed by some that deep in the solar interior, when the Sun was young, free-moving protons struck the lithium and changed it into helium. There are scientists who question this explanation since such a change would be most unusual; but under the extreme conditions that exist in a young, evolving star curious changes might occur.

Right now astronomers are looking into the sky searching for lithium-rich stars—stars being born. They are watching a massive dust cloud in Orion that has recently been sending out huge amounts of infrared (long-wavelength) radiation. A few years ago the cloud may have been too cold to produce any radiation at all. It may be contracting, getting warmer, and in a few years more it may become a cool (4 000°) star—the early youth of a T Tauri star. Any day now you may read about it in your newspaper, just as people read about FU Orionis back in 1936.

O AND B ASSOCIATIONS

T Tauris are young stars that are still unstabilized. They will settle down eventually and become main-sequence stars; pressure outward will equal pressure inward. Energy will be radiated steadily for billions of years.

Other types of young stars have lifetimes that cover only a few million years. These short-lived stars are placed at the far left of the main sequence, meaning they are very hot (blue or blue-white) and very massive. They are known as O or B type stars.

When stars began to be classified, the brightest and most massive were called A stars, the next brightest and most massive were called B, and so on. Later, when better measuring instruments became available and more was known about stars, it was found that O stars were the most luminous; then came B stars. A stars were in third place. Now the letter designations of the stars, in order of decreasing mass, temperature, and luminosity, are O, B, A, F, G, K, M. You can remember the order by the catch phrase: "Oh, Be A Fine Girl, Kiss Me"—a device supposedly originated by students at Harvard University.

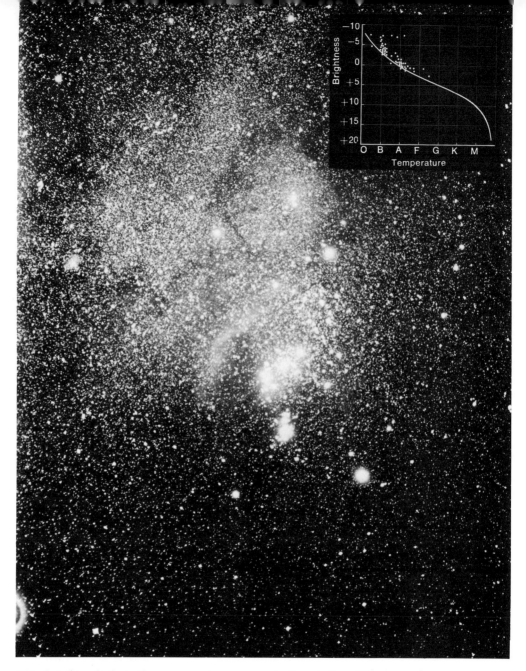

This bright nebula in Orion contains an association of O and B type stars.
The graph shows the position of such stars in relation to the main sequence.
(Hale Observatories)

You recall that T Tauri stars are embedded in clouds of interstellar dust and gases. They result when these materials pack together under the effects of gravitation. Similarly, O and B stars are found in associations, or groups of several of them, and surrounded by interstellar dust and gas clouds. (The density of the gas is about 10,000 times the density of the space surrounding the material, which is only 0.1 particle per cubic centimeter.) A typical representation of these stars is found in the constellation Orion.

Motion through space is a common condition of all stars. It has been computed that the stars in an O association are moving so fast that in about 100 million years they will be so dispersed that the association will no longer be apparent. Therefore any association that is observed must be considerably less than 100 million years old —a very short period when compared with the billions of years that make the lifetimes of other main-sequence stars.

What would cause stars to move away from the location where they were formed? One theory suggests that the original cloud formation may have been 10 or so light years across, and that the gases toward the center of the formation (enough to make thousands of stars) packed together, became very hot, and expanded rapidly. Gases toward the edges of the cloud would be cooler. The hot gases moving outward compressed the cooler gases into a shell or layer in which stars formed. The expansion of the hot gases persisted, driving the newly formed stars farther apart, and the motion continues today.

This theory fits well for some associations that have been observed. But it does not fit all of them—the Orion association for example. Studies of three stars quite removed from the Orion group indicate that they were originally part of the group, having been formed about 3 million years ago. Two of the stars, AE Aurigae and Mu Columbae,

The three named stars were probably at one time part of the Orion association of stars.

AE Aurigae

53 Arietis

Mu Columbae

are traveling very fast—about 130 kilometers per second—and in exactly opposite directions. A third star, 53 Arietis, is moving at about 70 kilometers per second. Other stars in the association, however, have a speed of only about 8 kilometers per second. Perhaps these three stars originated in some tremendous explosive event and, once set in motion, have continued to move fast. Another theory holds that when they were formed, at the same time, they were set in motion by action-reaction, somewhat as with a rocket: the rocket moves ahead while the fuel gases move in the opposite direction. One of the stars may be the "rocket," and the second star may be the "exhaust gases."

Yet another theory supposes that each of the runaway stars may at one time have been part of a double-star system—two stars moving around each other. One of the stars may have exploded and blown itself apart in two fragments. The other star may have continued to move through space at the same velocity it had when it was revolving around the companion star.

Astronomers continue to observe O and B type associations. So far about eighty of them have been discovered. They hope to learn enough about them to understand why the stars move as they do, and why some seem to be runaway stars. There are many questions to be answered about these stars.

But astronomers have a lot of the answers too. They know that the O and B stars are three and four times more massive than the Sun and that they reach surface temperatures of as much as 30 000°K. (You recall that the temperature of the Sun's surface is about 6 000°K.) Also, it is known that these rare massive stars are in the main sequence, which means they are converting hydrogen to helium. But they cannot stay there very long—only about 10 million years or

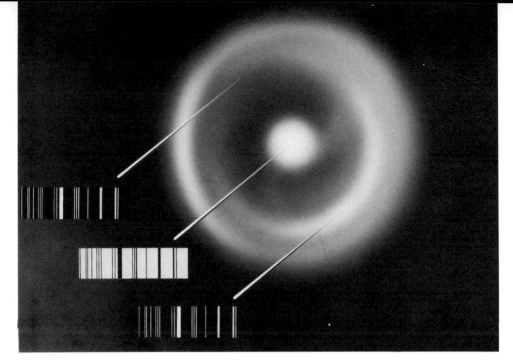

Both bright and dark lines are seen in the spectra of O and B type stars.

so, a fraction of the billions of years the Sun is spending in the main sequence. That's because they use up their hydrogen a million times faster than the Sun does.

Associations such as we've been discussing always contain stars that show bright lines in their spectra. These bright emission lines mean that the stars have very hot and extensive atmospheres. The atmospheres extend so far out from the stars that we can see the bright lines produced by the hot gases. Dark lines also show up, these being produced by the passage of radiation through the atmosphere that lies between the star and us.

T Tauris and O and B associations are young stars: gases that have just started their life cycles. Stars that have passed through their lifetimes and have reached old age are equally interesting and extraordinary.

AGEING STARS

RED GIANTS

When a star, such as the Sun, is in the main sequence, it is a hydrogen-burning star; hydrogen is fusing to produce helium. After some 10 billion years much of the helium that has been produced will be concentrated at the center of the star. No heat is produced there by nuclear reactions; gravitation takes over, packing the helium together, and the temperature goes up because of gravitation.

The hydrogen remaining in the star forms into a shell surrounding the helium core. Heat from the core warms up the hydrogen shell, and once again nuclear reactions (hydrogen to helium) begin. The fusion process in the hydrogen shell occurs much more rapidly than it did when the star was younger, because additional heat is now supplied from the helium core of the star.

We know that as temperature increases, a star becomes brighter. That is true when the energy can escape. But in an ageing star, most of the heat from the core is absorbed by the hydrogen shell. Also, great amounts of heat are consumed as the star becomes larger. Because less heat is radiated into space the star does not become brighter; its luminosity remains about the same.

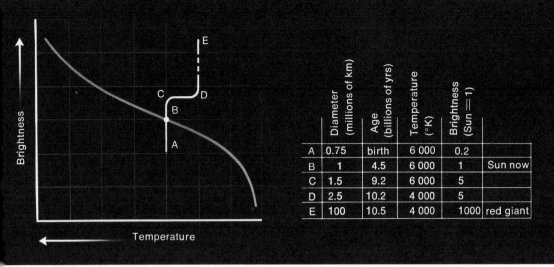

	Diameter (millions of km)	Age (billions of yrs)	Temperature (°K)	Brightness (Sun = 1)	
A	0.75	birth	6 000	0.2	
B	1	4.5	6 000	1	Sun now
C	1.5	9.2	6 000	5	
D	2.5	10.2	4 000	5	
E	100	10.5	4 000	1000	red giant

Ten and a half billion years in the life history of a star like the Sun, from birth (A) to red giant (E). Vertical progressions from A to C and from D to E show increases in brightness; horizontal progression from C to D shows a drop in temperature. When the Sun becomes a red giant, it will have a diameter of some 100 million kilometers and will be a thousand times brighter than it is now.

Because the star is expanding, the energy radiated is lost from a much greater surface, and the amount released from any given unit of surface is less. Surface temperature therefore drops to about 4 000°K, which means the star becomes reddish.

As more helium is produced, the core gets more compressed and hotter. The increase in heat speeds up the hydrogen-burning process. This makes more heat, which is what causes expansion of the star. But the gases in the star cannot absorb all of this heat, so a large part of it begins to reach the surface and is radiated into space. In other words, the brightness of the star increases rapidly. The star becomes more luminous and larger; it has evolved into a red giant.

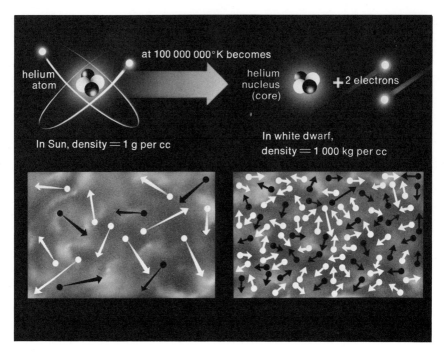

at 100 000 000°K becomes

helium
atom

helium
nucleus
(core) **+** 2 electrons

In Sun, density = 1 g per cc

In white dwarf,
density = 1 000 kg per cc

*In the Sun, protons and electrons move freely. In a white dwarf, the protons
and electrons are restricted; matter has become degenerate.*

Temperature continues to rise in the helium core—up and up it
goes, finally reaching 100 000 000°K. At this temperature a fusion
reaction begins that changes helium into carbon. The star has become
a helium-fusion reactor. Brightness does not continue to increase,
however; instead, the star becomes dimmer. This is why.

The helium is now compressed so much, packed so tightly together,
that a teaspoonful of it would weigh several tons. This pressure and
the high temperature break apart the helium atoms into helium cores
(double protons) and electrons. When free electrons are packed together tightly, they reach a point where they can be compressed no
further. The helium core, while it is still a gas, acts as though it were

a solid. We say that the matter has become degenerate: it does not behave normally.

Temperature keeps building up because of helium fusion, and because of hydrogen fusion in the shell. But because the core acts as a solid, it cannot expand gently as a gas does and so dissipate the increased heat. It just gets hotter. The hotter core speeds up the fusion reaction. This adds to the heat; one condition feeds the other. After a few hours of this build-up, the nuclear reactions occur so fast that the star has become a nuclear bomb—the red giant explodes, blowing off its outer layers.

Actually it is the helium core that explodes. It cannot expand in any other way than explosively. The heat is dissipated, so the temperature at the core drops; so does the temperature of the hydrogen shell. Remember, a star is maintained by outward expansion caused by heating, and inward packing caused by gravitation. Packing is now the dominant force, and so the star contracts. Once again the helium core is compressed, but not nearly as much as just before the explosion occurred. The helium produces heat and carbon. When the heat cannot be absorbed further the core expands. It can do this now because it is not degenerate—it is not compressed to the point where it acts like a solid. The expansion causes cooling, and the reaction goes on evenly. Now the star is in equilibrium; it is a balanced helium-burning star.

Carbon is being produced, and after a while there will be no more helium at the core of the star. The star that used to have a helium core will now have a carbon core. Surrounding that core there will still be helium, however. The carbon core now becomes a nuclear reactor. Its temperature reaches perhaps 600 000 000°, producing new elements. The star expands and the temperature in the outer

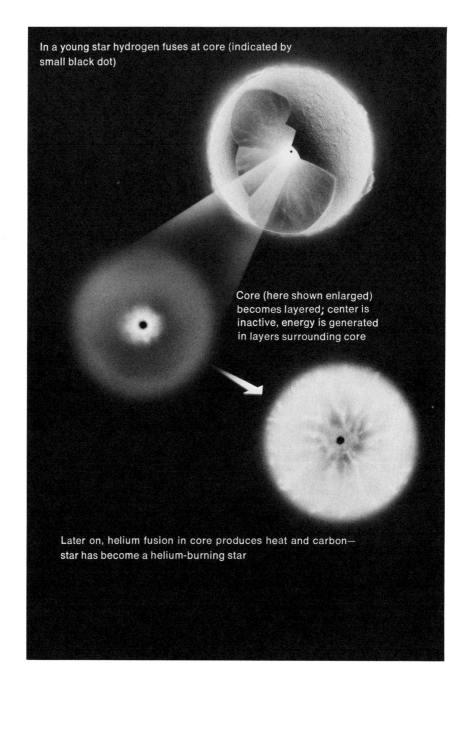

In a young star hydrogen fuses at core (indicated by small black dot)

Core (here shown enlarged) becomes layered; center is inactive, energy is generated in layers surrounding core

Later on, helium fusion in core produces heat and carbon—star has become a helium-burning star envelope dips, but the star becomes brighter. Its surface temperature is lower but its size is much greater, so the total radiation is much greater than before. Once again it moves into a red giant phase—a bright red giant.

In a well-advanced supergiant star the core is essentially iron. The remaining nuclear fuels are arranged in shells, where fusion reactions continue— hydrogen to helium, helium to carbon, carbon to silicon, silicon to iron. Density is very low (little more than a hot vacuum), and the surface is not sharply defined.

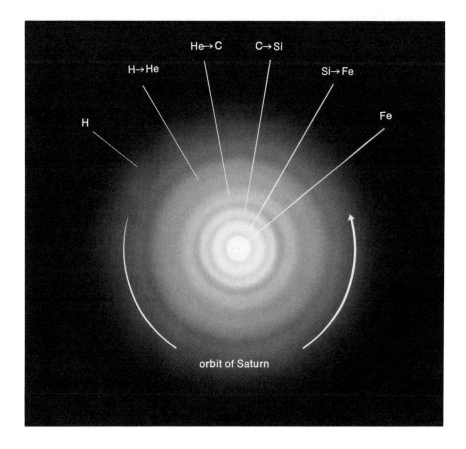

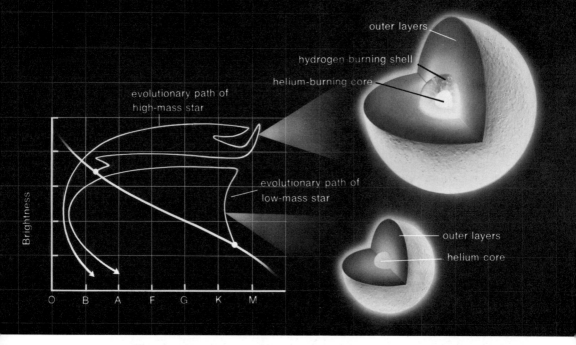

A high-mass star ages rapidly to the red-giant stage. Then helium is converted to carbon. As energy is depleted, the star becomes a white dwarf.

A low-mass star becomes a red giant also. It is never hot enough however, for the helium-to-carbon process. After a long, slow evolution it becomes a white dwarf.

Further expansion will result in cooling. Cooling will be followed by contraction. The star's core will heat up again but, since it is much smaller now, the temperature will not get high enough for nuclear reactions to resume. The star will pass out of the main sequence. Luminosity will become less and less; temperature will drop rapidly; and the star's destiny will be determined, for the star will have expended its energy. It will become a white dwarf—still giving off heat for millions of years but cooling inevitably.

Stars that are more massive or less massive than the sun have somewhat different endings, it is believed. Those more massive may blow themselves apart in cosmic explosions of incredible magnitude; or they may retain much of their mass and collapse to become black holes in space. Those less massive last much longer and reach old age more quietly.

PLANETARY NEBULAS

The amount of heat generated by gravitation depends upon the mass of the star. In stars slightly less massive than the Sun, the temperature never reaches 600 000 000°K—the temperature needed to start carbon fusion reactions. However, there is enough compression to raise the temperature of the carbon core enough to heat the helium shell surrounding it and thus speed up fusion in the shell. This causes expansion of the envelope of the star; the star becomes a red giant.

Expansion continues and, as the star gets larger, it also becomes cooler. When the gases are cool enough, electrons combine with protons and atoms are produced. When an electron combines with a proton, a small unit of energy called a photon is set free. The photon moves only a small distance before it is captured by an atom.

The energy that is released causes the envelope of the star to heat and expand further. As the gases expand, they cool; more protons and electrons combine, more heat energy is produced, causing still further expansion. Eventually the envelope breaks free of the star core, forming a huge sphere of gas, which may have a temperature of 100 000°, surrounding the central star.

When this process began, we saw the star as a red giant—we were observing the outer envelope. Now, when the envelope separates from the core, the core itself can be observed. It is so hot that much of its radiant energy is in the ultraviolet region—light that is invisible. However, the ultraviolet energy is picked up by the gases in the shell and reradiated as visible light. The sphere of gases shows yellowish nearest the star because of the greater energy there, changing to reddish as distance from the star increases and energy level drops.

When astronomers first observed these round gaseous formations through early telescopes, they appeared as small, blue-green disks that resembled the planets Uranus and Neptune, and so they were called planetary nebulas. Some scientists thought they were looking at material from which planets would evolve. Even though we know that such formations are not planets, nor birthplaces of planets, we still call them by that name. A beautiful example of a planetary nebula is shown in the photograph below.

M-57, the Ring Nebula in Lyra. The core long ago threw off the shell of gases, which now surrounds the central star. It appears thicker at the outside because there we are looking edgewise through the gases. *(Hale Observatories)*

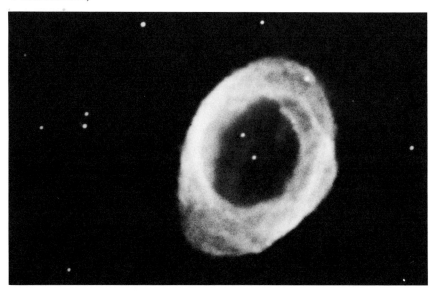

WHITE DWARFS

After a star has lost its outer envelope, the core of the star (the carbon core and the helium shell around the carbon) remains active. The carbon core collapses. The helium shell produces heat, most of which is radiated into space but some of which is taken up by the carbon. The carbon, however, is made of free protons and electrons—and free electrons (degenerate matter) act as a solid and cannot be compressed beyond a given point. Therefore there is a limit to the temperature that can be attained; it never gets to 600 000 000°, the temperature needed for carbon to start fusing into heavier elements. The packing together of material in the carbon core ends when the density is so high that a teaspoonful would weigh about 10 tons. At that point the star is only a bit larger than the Earth.

Gravity on such a star would be tremendous. Gravity increases with mass and with closeness to the center of the mass. For example, on the Earth's surface you weigh, let's say, about 45 kilograms (100 pounds). On one of these burned-out white dwarf stars (for that is what our star has become) you would weigh millions of kilograms, since the mass of the star is so great and its diameter so small.

The Sun's core of helium and hydrogen is surrounded by atoms that take up much of the heat generated in the interior. Therefore the outer part of the Sun is much cooler than the central core. If there were no atoms in the Sun, the surface temperature would be much higher—so high that the Earth and everything on it would be vaporized.

A white dwarf has no atoms. Its core of carbon and helium is essentially free protons and electrons—degenerate matter. This degenerate matter does not impede the movement of heat by radiation.

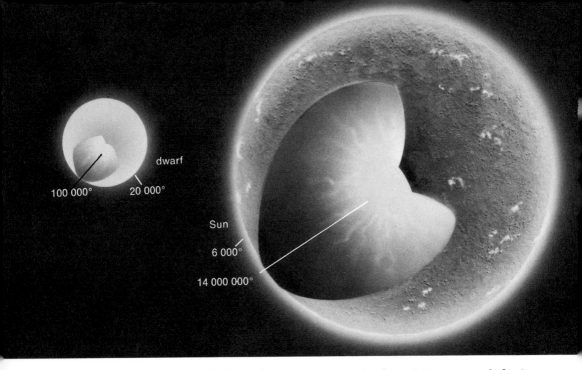

dwarf

100 000°　　20 000°

Sun

6 000°

14 000 000°

In a white dwarf the surface temperature is about 20 percent of the interior temperature. In the Sun the surface temperature is a small fraction of 1 percent of the interior temperature.

Therefore the temperature of the outer region of a dwarf star is not much less than the temperature of the central core.

As time passes, the star cools; more and more of its heat radiates into space. The white dwarf becomes a yellow dwarf. With further cooling its color changes to orange and then to red. It becomes dimmer and dimmer, and ends its existence as a black dwarf: a superdense burned-out ash, the last remnant of a once brilliant star.

PERIODIC VARIABLES—CEPHEIDS AND OTHERS

Many stars have their beginnings as T Tauris—unstable masses in the process of settling down. They then go through evolutionary changes.

They may follow different paths, but all lead inevitably to the death of the star, to its becoming a cold cinder. Along the way many stars become pulsating stars—stars that vary in brightness from year to year or day to day, in some cases from hour to hour.

Some of these stars vary erratically. That is, they may shine evenly for centuries or milleniums, then suddenly become brighter. The new brightness may be retained for hours, days, weeks; then the star returns to its original intensity. Other stars follow a rhythmic cycle, going from dimness to brightness to dimness in a regular fashion. Such stars are called periodic variables.

There are three important classes of these stars. Those with pulsation periods of more than 100 days are long-period variables. The best known example is one called Mira in the constellation Cetus, the Whale. This is a constellation that appears low in southern skies during winter months in the Northern Hemisphere. Mira was the first true variable star to be observed. For three and a half centuries men have noticed its appearance in a part of the sky that is usually dark. At its dimmest, Mira cannot be seen with the unaided eye. During a pulsation, its brightness increases at least one hundred times. It is a red supergiant, at least ten times more massive than the Sun and with a diameter of some 450 million kilometers. Its density is very low, however, being about one three-millionth that of the Sun.

The name Mira (which in Latin means "Marvelous") was given the star in 1596 by the German astronomer David Fabricius (1564–1617) when he discovered that the star was variable. It has a period of 330 days. After about 10 days of maximum brightness Mira begins to fade slowly, taking about seven months to reach its dimmest stage. Then a slow climb of some three months to maximum brightness begins.

A second class of variables are called cepheids. They are named after Delta Cephei, which is typical of the group. The periods of these stars, which range between one day and fifty days, are very regular. They are all supergiant stars—much larger than the Sun but having temperatures about the same as it has.

There are two types of cepheids. One group, called classical cepheids, is made up of stars that contain a lot of metal and are found generally along the plane of our galaxy. The second type of cepheids comprises those that occur among other stars in globular star clusters. These are formations of hundreds, thousands, even hundreds of thou-

Locations on the H-R diagram of the main types of variable stars.

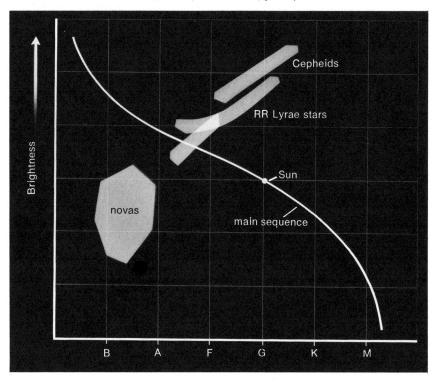

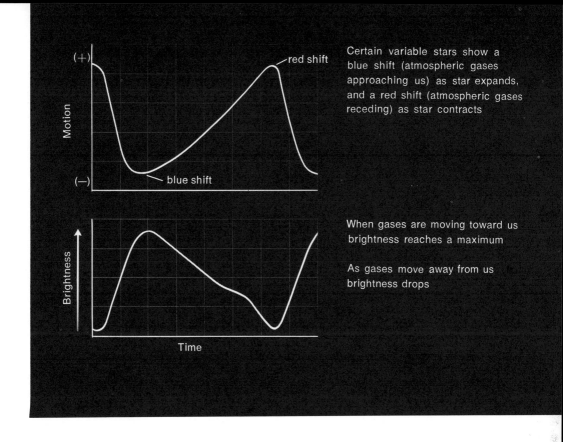

Certain variable stars show a blue shift (atmospheric gases approaching us) as star expands, and a red shift (atmospheric gases receding) as star contracts

When gases are moving toward us brightness reaches a maximum

As gases move away from us brightness drops

sands of stars, which move as a unit around the central region of the galaxy. There are believed to be about a hundred of these clusters. Cepheid variables enable us to measure distances to stars that are very far away—as we'll find out shortly. First let's consider the third class of periodic variables.

Those stars that have very short periods of variation—not more than one day—are called RR Lyrae stars. Like the Type II cepheids, they occur in globular clusters. On the H-R diagram they are placed above the main sequence, meaning they are large stars; and they are placed toward the left, meaning they are white-hot. As you can see, RR Lyrae stars are found in a very limited, narrow section of the diagram.

Brightness decreases with distance. At the left, two lamps of the same brightness appear to be different when they are at different distances.

When a dim object (the candle) is closer to us than an object that is actually much brighter, the dimmer object appears to be the brighter.

WHY DO STARS PULSATE?

Over several decades the light of variable stars has been studied and measured in a multitude of ways. When changes in luminosity are plotted against time, a light-curve diagram is produced. If the light is passed through a spectroscope, there is a Doppler shift toward the blue as the star brightens, and a shift toward the red as the star becomes dimmer. When the Doppler shifts of the light are plotted, the curve that results is almost an exact mirror image of the light curve.

Because of these periodic Doppler shifts, astronomers know that something is actually moving first toward them (the blue shift) and then away from them (the red shift). Apparently the whole outer atmosphere of the star expands, and the part in our line of sight

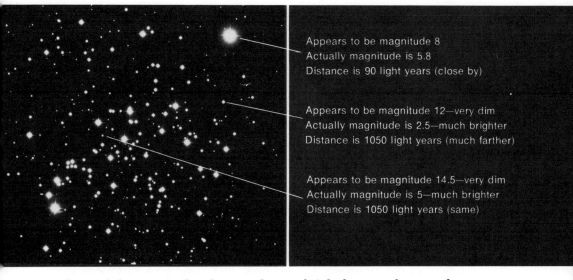

Appears to be magnitude 8
Actually magnitude is 5.8
Distance is 90 light years (close by)

Appears to be magnitude 12—very dim
Actually magnitude is 2.5—much brighter
Distance is 1050 light years (much farther)

Appears to be magnitude 14.5—very dim
Actually magnitude is 5—much brighter
Distance is 1050 light years (same)

Some of the stars in the photograph seem bright because they are close to us. Some of the dim stars are actually much brighter. They appear dim because of their great distance from us. (Hale Observatories)

moves toward us. When it reaches maximum expansion, the atmosphere holds there momentarily, then collapses toward the center.

If this is so, as observations indicate, what could happen in the atmosphere of a star to make it pack together and then fly apart so regularly? The answer is not known. However, we do know that all stars must expand a bit and contract in order to remain stable. You recall that in a normal, steady star, thermal expansion and gravitational contraction must be in balance. Slight adjustments must be made in order to keep this so. In a periodic variable star, a similar expansion to maintain stability very likely occurs. If the expansion continued beyond the point of stability, internal forces would bring the gases back toward the center. This counteraction may go farther than necessary. Then the process would start all over again.

Just as a ball on the end of an elastic will oscillate up and down for a short time but must eventually settle down, so also must a star, it would seem. The pulsations could not go on for an indefinite period (as we believe occurs in variables) but would have to end when stability was reached. However, there may be combinations of conditions of temperatures, mass, and composition within certain stars that enable the pulsations to continue. If so, these qualities would apply to only a few stars, and so periodic variables would be limited to a narrow region of the H-R diagram—as we've seen they are. Most stars, if they have ever been pulsating stars, have not been able to maintain the periodic expansion-contraction and now appear elsewhere on the diagram. It is believed that some such history is associated with stars that are more massive than the Sun.

DISTANCES TO PULSATING STARS

One way to determine the distance to a star is by measuring how bright the star appears against how bright it really is. Let's use candles to explain how this works. If a candle is 5 meters from you, it is of a certain brightness. If another candle is placed 10 meters from you, or twice as far, it will appear only one quarter as bright as the first candle. As distance increases, we know, brightness decreases. Suppose there is a third candle. We do not know how far away it is, but we know it appears only one sixteenth as bright as the nearby candle. We could then figure it is four times farther, or 20 meters, away. This is the method of finding distances to the stars.

A star may appear very dim. If we know how bright that star would be if it were close by, we have an indication of how far away it has to be to appear as dim as it does. In the 1920s, for instance, astrono-

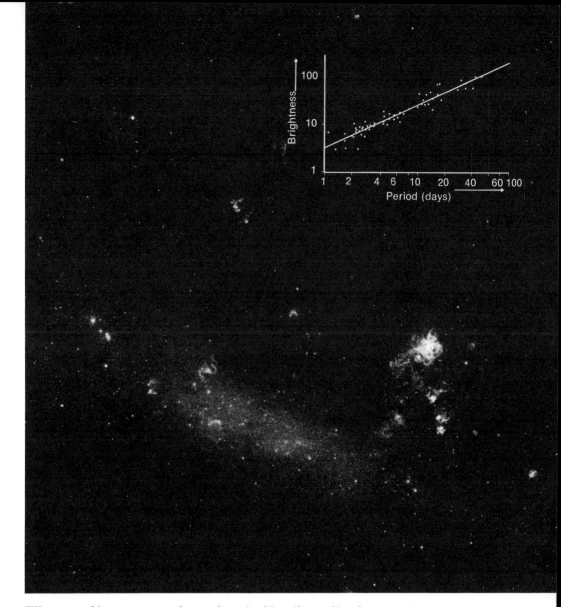

When variable stars were observed in the Magellanic Clouds, it was found that as the pulsation period increased, so did the apparent brightness. Since all the stars in these clouds are at essentially the same distance from us, it became possible to relate period to real brightness. The relationship became a key for finding distances to other star systems and galaxies. (Cerro Tololo Observatory)

mers were able to determine the distance to the Magellanic Clouds, two galaxies visible from the Southern Hemisphere. Careful observations revealed that there are many cepheid variable stars in the Clouds. Astronomers also knew there are cepheid variable stars of known distance in globular clusters associated with our own galaxy.

It was discovered that there is a direct relationship between the period of a cepheid variable and its real, or actual, brightness. Thereupon it became possible to apply the "candle yardstick." Learn the period of a cepheid, and from the period you can get the actual brightness. Observe the star to determine how bright it appears to be. With these two pieces of information (the actual brightness and the apparent brightness) an astronomer can determine the distance to any cepheid variable, whether in our own galaxy or in another galaxy thousands of light years from us, by comparing it with a cepheid of known distance.

This procedure had a trap in it—one that created a major error in astronomy that was not corrected until 1952. It was believed that all cepheids, both the classical and the globular-cluster types, behaved in the same way. That is, both types of cepheids would have the same brightness if their periods were the same. In 1952 it was found that this is not so: in fact a globular-cluster cepheid with a period equal to that of a classical cepheid will be about four times dimmer.

When astronomers first studied cepheids in photographs of the Andromeda Galaxy, they computed that the formation was about a million light years away. With the knowledge that lone classical cepheids are actually much brighter than had been thought, it became necessary to revise the estimate. With present-day knowledge, it is now believed that the Andromeda Galaxy is over 2 million light years away. Hence in 1952 new knowledge of cepheid variable stars

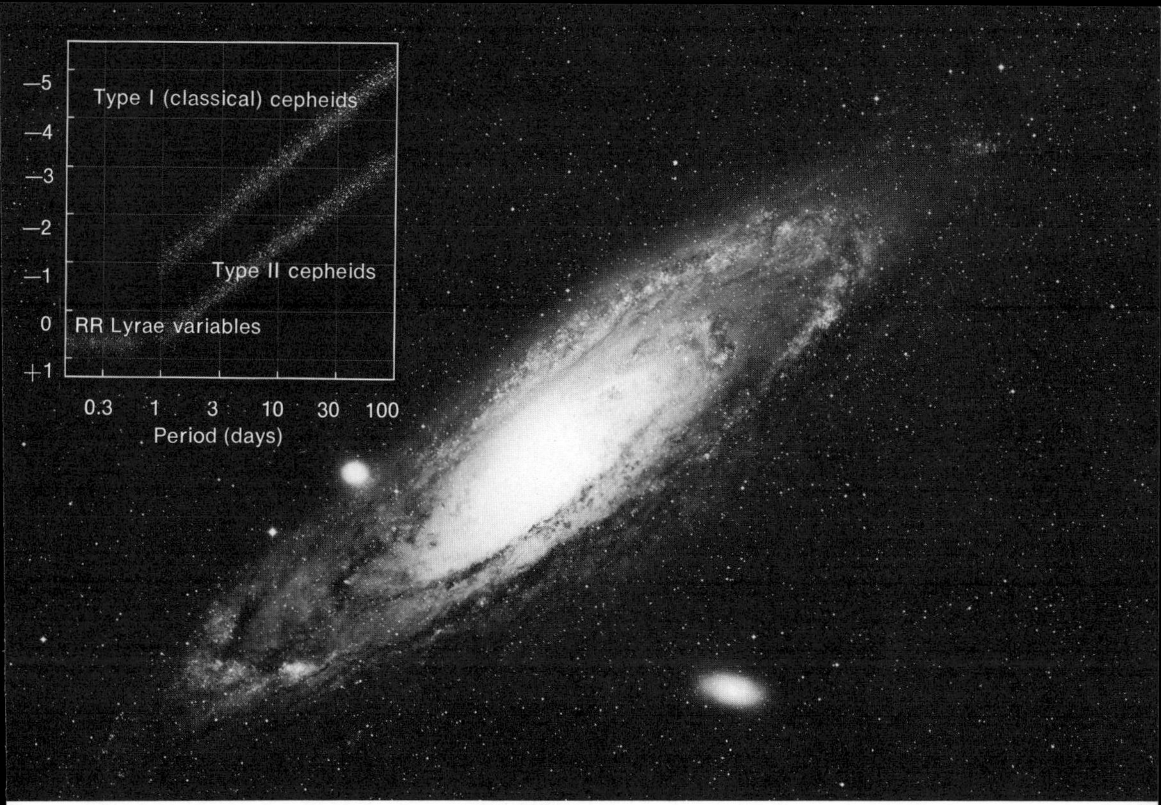

−5
−4
−3
−2
−1
0
+1
Type I (classical) cepheids
Type II cepheids
RR Lyrae variables
0.3
1
3
10
30
100
Period (days)

The periods of cepheids observed in the Andromeda Galaxy revealed their actual brightness. Knowing apparent brightness and real brightness, it was possible to determine the distance to the galaxy—some 2,100,000 light years. (Hale Observatories)

resulted in doubling man's conception of the size of the universe. Cepheids remain extremely important "yardsticks" for measuring the vast distances to galaxies beyond our own.

In addition to the three main classes of periodic variables, there are many other types of variable stars. There are cool, red flare stars that erupt periodically, producing tremendous amounts of radio energy. There are extremely hot stars that have unsteady periods. There are also explosive variable stars, or novas.

EXPLODING STARS—
NOVAS AND SUPERNOVAS

To the casual viewer of the sky, the stars seem to be always the same. Their relative locations in the constellations appear unchanging; so does their brightness. Also, there seem to be always the same number of stars—no new ones have appeared, and no old stars have disappeared.

But none of these conditions is true; stars do move, old stars do go out of existence (and some young stars also). New stars appear, too —stars that have not been seen because of their dimness and that suddenly flare up. Because these stars had not been seen before, and because the reason for their occurrence was not understood, they were called novae or novas—new stars, after the Latin word for "new."

It is estimated that in any given year perhaps a hundred novas occur in our galaxy. Because many of them are at locations that cannot be observed even with telescopes, we see perhaps five or six in a year. Some of these novas become bright in just a few hours and then take two or three days to quiet down. At their brightest they may be about a hundred times brighter than before the increase. Such stars are called dwarf novas.

Ordinary novas get much brighter—the brightest stage may be a

Novas appear to be double stars in which gases from the larger star flow into the smaller one. The process reverses as distribution of mass changes.

hundred thousand times greater than the dim stage—and the maximum is reached in a day or so.

NOVAS AND WHITE DWARFS

Novas occupy an area of the H-R diagram that is below and to the left of the main sequence. This means that they are hotter than the Sun and less bright; they must have a smaller surface. It is believed that the white dwarf stage that comes later in a star's history is common to all stars. Yet not all stars pass through the nova stage to become quiet white dwarfs. What is there about novas that is different from other stars?

It is believed the essential difference is that novas have another star associated with them. Novas seem to be double, or binary, stars. From those that have been studied, the following description seems to be typical. The nova itself, the star that is exploding, is a variable white dwarf—a star that explodes maybe once or twice in a hundred years. The mass of the white dwarf is about one fourth that of the Sun, and its diameter about one hundredth of the Sun's diameter. The white dwarf's mass is about 80,000 times the Earth's mass, and its diameter is about 16 000 kilometers, a bit larger than the diameter of the Earth. Associated with this unsettled white dwarf is a dim red star, one having about the same mass as the dwarf but a diameter a hundred times greater than that of the Sun—meaning a diameter of some 150 million kilometers.

The two stars compose a two-body system, much as the Earth and Moon do. In the case of the Earth-Moon, the two bodies revolve around each other, or around a center of balance of the system. The center is about 1 600 kilometers below the Earth's surface. In the double-star system, the center of balance is slightly within the red star. The stars move around each other very fast, taking about six hours to complete one revolution. Gases from the red star flow into the region surrounding the small white dwarf star; they make an envelope around the star. Some of the gases probably escape into space, lost forever to the system. Also, some of the gases are attracted to the surface of the small star.

For this to happen, one of the stars must have had slightly more mass than the other star in their early age. As they became older, the more massive star burned up fuel more rapidly than did the other star. When about 10 percent of the star's hydrogen had been consumed (converted to helium), the more massive star began to expand. As it did so, the star became redder. When it had expanded so much that the center of the system was inside the red star, gases from it flowed into the region around the white star.

As the more massive star lost hydrogen, its ageing process speeded up. Gravitation contracted the gases; they packed together tighter and tighter, and the large, dim red star became smaller—it became a white dwarf. Meanwhile the small white or blue-white star had been gaining material, which had caused its ageing process to slow down. Eventually, however, nuclear reactions in this star used up the newly added material. The star expanded, grew cooler and redder. It got large enough to lose material to the newly created dwarf star (and to space). And so the reaction continues—over billions of years: first one star is the loser of material (a large red star), then it becomes a gainer of material (a small blue-white dwarf).

Although such changes are occurring in the system, we still do not know why novas explode—why they suddenly increase in brightness. Perhaps the gases piling up on the surface produce some sort of instability that can be eliminated only by a violent reaction. Then a shell of hot, bright gases, with a mass about one ten-thousandth of the Sun's mass, is ejected from the surface. It speeds away at 1 600 kilometers per second. Some of these gases escape from the system. But a considerable part of them is retained by the dwarf, and the changes described above continue. Ultimately the two stars in the system settle down to become quiet white dwarf stars. Then they cool further and become black dwarfs. But the process requires billions of years, a longer period of time than the age of our galaxy. It is questionable if there are any black dwarfs in the Milky Way Galaxy.

SUPERNOVAS

Although there may be an increase of a hundred thousand times in the brightness of a nova, still most of these events cannot be seen with the unaided eye; the stars are too far away and the brightness is not great enough. Not so with supernovas. These are cataclysmic explosions during which a star may increase in brightness a million times or more—a hundred million times brighter than the Sun. The star literally blows itself apart, losing 50 percent or more of its mass to space and retaining little of its former nature.

Compared with the frequency of the novas we've been discussing, supernovas are rare events. It has been estimated that in any given galaxy there are only three in a thousand years. In our own galaxy only three have been observed. Tycho Brahe (1546–1601), the famous Danish astronomer, reported in 1572 that he had seen a "new" star in the constellation Cassiopeia. A year later he published his observations in a book called *De Nova Stella* ("*Concerning the New Star*"). Since that time a star appearing to explode into bril-

Tycho's Star of 1572 appeared in the constellation Cassiopeia.

liance has been called a nova. In his report Tycho wrote: "I was so astonished at this sight that I was not ashamed to doubt the trustworthiness of my eyes." After many observations and measurements he concluded that "this star is not some kind of comet or fiery meteor, whether these be generated beneath the Moon or above the Moon, but . . . is a star shining in the firmament itself; one that has never previously been seen before our time, in any age since the beginning of the world." On November 15, 1572, the star was as bright as Venus (magnitude —4). Two months later it had dimmed to about the brightness of Sirius, and two months after that it had disappeared. When at its brightest, the star was perhaps a billion times brighter than it had been before Tycho saw it. Tycho was twenty-six years old, and his observations of Tycho's Star, as it came to be called, gave him a prominent place among astronomers.

Kepler's Star of 1604 appeared in the constellation Ophiuchus.

Thirty-two years later, Johannes Kepler (1571–1630), who had been a student of Tycho, saw another "new" star. This one was in the constellation Ophiuchus. It became as bright as Jupiter, which would be magnitude −2. For seventeen months beginning on September 30, 1604, the star could be observed.

Tycho's Star of 1572 and Kepler's of 1604 are the only two supernovas in our galaxy that have been recorded in the Western Hemisphere. However, in 1054 the Chinese reported a "new" star in the constellation Taurus—one so bright it could be seen in daytime. Curiously there are no European records of the 1054 event. An explanation for this is hard to find; perhaps it is because the event occurred during the Dark Ages, a period of minimal intellectual activity. Even so, one would think there must have been individuals who saw the star, and who recognized its importance and so recorded their observations. It appears that there were none—although ancient drawings found in caves and canyons in northern Arizona suggest that American Indians living at that time saw the star. A circle and a crescent in the drawings probably depict the Moon and a nearby bright star. Astronomers' calculations reveal that the supernova was very close to the Moon on July 5, 1054. Anthropologists believe Indians were living in that region sometime between 900 and 1100, so it is possible this is the only record in the Western world of the event recorded by the Chinese in 1054.

Much later, in the latter part of the eighteenth century, Charles Messier (1730–1817), the French astronomer, discovered a gaseous formation (a nebula) near Zeta Tauri, the star forming the tip of the lower horn of Taurus, the Bull. Actually the discovery of the nebula had been made in 1731 by John Bevis, an English physician, but was forgotten. The report and drawings Bevis made were never printed because the printer who had been hired went bankrupt. Messier's rediscovery in 1758 was recorded. It became the first of some hundred faint objects—nebulas and clusters—that Messier was to catalogue.

As telescopes became more efficient, details of such nebulas were gradually revealed. In 1844, with a 72-inch reflecting telescope, the Irish astronomer William Parsons, the third Earl of Rosse (1800–1867), studied Messier's nebula carefully. He was able to see not only the central mass but also numerous ragged filaments of light. He was reminded of a crab's body and its extended legs, and so called the formation the Crab Nebula—the name it retains today.

You cannot see the nebula with the unaided eye, although you can imagine its location, as shown in the illustration, when viewing the

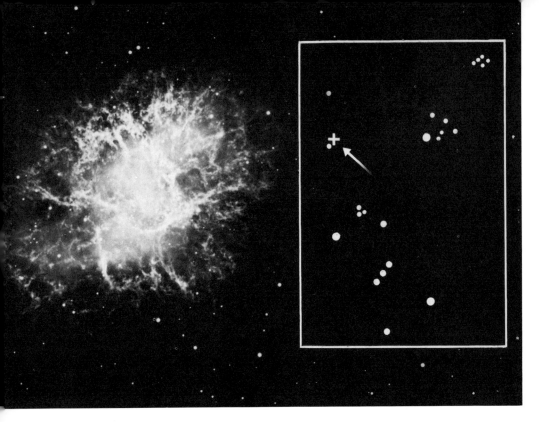

The Crab Nebula in Taurus is a fascinating laboratory of astronomy. (Hale Observatories)

skies of a winter night. It is a bit north and west of Orion in the constellation Taurus, which is identifiable by the V-shaped formation of stars and the small, tight cluster called the Pleiades. One might think of the V as the nose of the bull, the Pleiades as his shoulder. Extending outward from the V are the horns of the bull, the lower one terminating in the star Zeta Tauri. Just above that star lies the Crab Nebula, an area that astronomers have observed more extensively than any other single formation. It has been called by Herbert Friedman, an astronomer who pioneered in the use of rocket-borne equipment, "one of the most marvelous pieces of architecture in the Universe." It is much too dim to be seen without a telescope. But modern astronomers have observed it regularly, and from careful study have obtained information of what happens when a star explodes.

There appear to be two main types of supernovas. Type I supernovas are explosions of old stars that have about as much mass as the Sun. They release more energy than Type II explosions. The Type II supernovas are explosions of massive young stars in the upper left portion of the H-R diagram. They occur in the spiral arms of the galaxy.

A Type I explosion occurs because of the behavior of degenerate matter—matter under such tremendous pressure that a cubic centimeter weighs two tons or so. In degenerate matter, you recall, most of the electrons are "frozen" into position; they do not move about. When the matter picks up temperature, it does not expand. Therefore the temperature increase is not dissipated by expansion and the resultant cooling. The increased temperature accelerates the rate of nuclear reactions. This causes further increase in temperature, which speeds up nuclear reactions, which increases temperature. The result is a fantastic explosion—one that blows the star apart, in some cases leaving only 10 percent of the original mass.

In a Type II supernova explosion, the interior temperature rises to more than 7 billion degrees. This happens because hydrogen, helium, and even heavier elements have been used up. The star contracts because of gravitation, and as it shrinks, temperature rises rapidly. Above 7 billion degrees nuclear reactions occur that consume energy rather than releasing it. The core shrinks rapidly to meet this demand for energy. Within seconds the outer part of the star collapses and crashes into the center. The lighter elements of the star, heated by the collapse, react rapidly, producing incredible heat. There

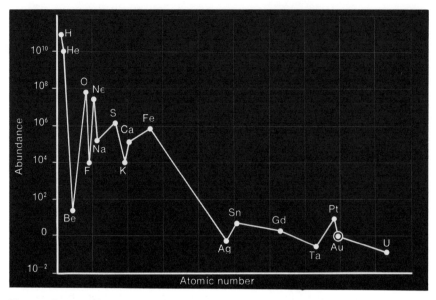

Using the incidence of gold as a base, the abundance of some of the elements in the universe is compared. Elements lighter than iron are relatively abundant. Heavier elements are relatively scarce; it is these elements that are produced in supernova explosions.

is no way to dissipate it, so the star explodes. Cosmic particles are thrown into space. So also is energy in all forms, from very powerful gamma rays and X rays to visible light, ultraviolet light, and radio waves. During the explosion protons and neutrons fly about, and many are captured by the nuclei of other atoms. In fleeting moments they build up to become heavier elements—those beyond iron. The time for these changes is so short and the energy expenditure so great the heavy elements never become abundant. In a table of the incidence of elements in the universe, the drop-off in those beyond iron is very steep.

All of this happened in the Crab Nebula some 7000 years ago (although because of its great distance it was not seen on the Earth until 900 years ago); and it is still extremely active. The gaseous formation is now 6 light years across, and the gases are still moving outward at speeds of some 1 500 kilometers an hour. The amount of energy contained in the particles that make up these gases is stupendous—probably equal to all the energy given off by the Sun in the past million years.

Some of the energy is in the form of ultraviolet light, which reveals the presence of hydrogen, helium, oxygen, sulfur, and other elements. A great deal of the energy is in the form of radio waves. As radio astronomers learned more about how radio waves are generated in a gaseous formation, they realized that the Crab Nebula is a puzzler. The nature of the radio waves is such that they had to be generated in some unusual fashion. In the 1950s it was suggested that they were produced by electrons moving at high speed along magnetic lines of force, a phenomenon called synchrotron radiation (the name comes from the synchrotron, a laboratory device that speeds up electrons to very high velocities). These electrons, when moving in a magnetic field, produce the radiation. Ordinarily photons (units of energy) are picked up and given off by atoms; consequently electrons of the atoms change position from one atomic shell to another. In synchrotron radiation, the photons are picked up and given off by the electrons alone. It is now believed that much of the energy of the Crab Nebula, light and gamma ray as well as radio, is produced in this fashion.

The Crab Nebula, then, is a gigantic synchrotron—a cosmic nuclear accelerator—releasing tremendous amounts of energy. But where does all the energy come from? Are the particles the ones produced in the original explosion? Have they been trapped for thousands of years, spiraling back and forth along the magnetic lines of force?

The wavelength of energy given off is determined by the level of energy of the electrons and the strength of the magnetic field. Light waves are very short compared with radio waves. The radio waves of the Crab are so long they can continue active for a hundred thousand years. But the optical electrons (those producing shorter-wave visible light) can continue for only a hundred years. Since they are still active (after thousands of years), there must be some way additional energy is supplied to them. It took many years, and many improvements of the technology of astronomy, to find how it is done.

But before the answer was found, X-ray astronomers added additional puzzlement. In the 1960s it was believed that X rays were produced by the Sun and other stars. Because X rays are dispersed by our atmosphere, one must get outside the atmosphere to "see" them. This has been done by sending out X-ray-sensitive equipment by rocket, by high-flying balloon, by satellite—and finally in manned space laboratories moving in orbit around the Earth. The Crab was identified as a powerful source of X rays by observing the nebula as the Moon passed in front of it. Rockets were launched just as the Moon was passing. Measurements dropped to zero when the Moon blocked the nebula, but the count went up again as soon as it had passed.

Calculations showed that the X rays were coming from a region of the Crab about 2 light years in diameter. And the X rays were very energetic—fifty times more so than the light radiation. The X rays were of such high energy that they could be produced for only a few months, or a year at the most. Also, it would seem that the X rays would lose their energy before escaping from the outer parts of the nebula. And it was hard to understand how their source could be 2 light years across if they all originated at a central location. Could there be several sources?

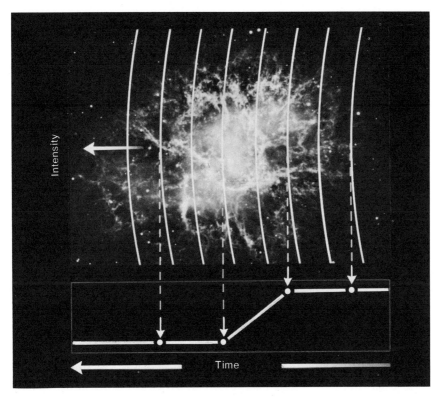

When the Moon passes in front of the Crab Nebula (from right to left), changes in X-ray intensity can be related to specific regions of the nebula. (Hale Observatories)

It was clear that the Crab Nebula is a remnant of an explosion of such magnitude we cannot comprehend it. Also, it was clear that the energy released is beyond explanation. Even so, theory told us that the light radiation should have diminished during the thousands of years that have passed since the event. But such was not the case. There was something pumping energy into the system. Astronomers were bewildered.

Then came the pulsars.

PULSARS—NEUTRON STARS

A pulsar (pulsating star) is a neutron star. It could be a remnant of a supernova explosion—the object that remains at the center of the sphere of expanding gases. It is also a stage beyond a white dwarf. You recall that a white dwarf is a star in which a mass equivalent to all the material in the Sun is packed into a volume about the size of the Earth, or even somewhat smaller. Density is therefore beyond comprehension—a cubic centimeter would weigh several tons. When the same amount of material is packed into a sphere only 16 kilometers across, a neutron star is created. Now the density is so tremendous that a marble-size volume would weigh more than 2 million tons.

In the original star from which the neutron star evolved, there were atoms. The diameter of one of these atoms is on the order of a hundred millionth of a centimeter. The parts of the atoms, mainly protons and neutrons, are called subatomic particles. The diameter of one of these particles is only ten trillionths of a centimeter, or one hundred-thousandth of the diameter of the atom. One hundred thousand of them side by side would be needed to stretch across the atom.

Atoms are three-dimensional, so let's think about the volume of an atom. It would be $100,000 \times 100,000 \times 100,000$ that of a single particle, or $1,000,000,000,000,000$ (1×10^{15}) times greater. In the most complex atom there are only about 300 subatomic particles. It is obvious that most of an atom is empty space. In a neutron star, it is believed, electrons have been pushed into protons, making them into neutrons. Also, gravitation has pulled the neutrons so tightly together they are touching. The empty space of the atom is now filled with neutrons, the massive parts of atoms. This is why density is so tremendous.

Before 1967, the discovery of neutron stars had been predicted by astronomers. They theorized that the stars would be massive but small, that they would rotate very rapidly, and that they would have very strong magnetic fields. In 1965 careful searches of the sky were started, especially in those regions where there had been supernovas,

Most of the volume of an atom is empty space. The massive core is very small. Eight atoms fill the space indicated below left.
In neutron stars massive cores are packed close together. Below right, the cores of eight atoms occupy a small proportion of the same space.

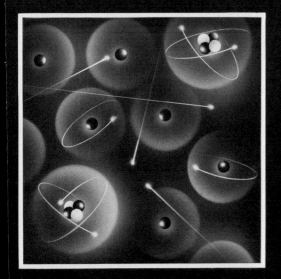
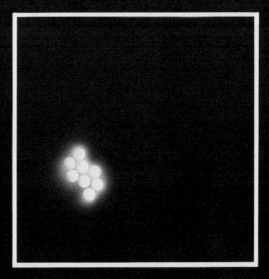

in the hope that observations of such stars might be made. But none was found, and astronomers turned to other matters.

In 1967 Jocelyn Bell, a student at Cambridge University in England, was assigned to get information about the radio waves coming from quasars—distant formations that have the mass of a galaxy but that appear star-like. As she scanned the sky, short radio pulses were picked up. They came from certain regions, and the bursts were regular, each lasting for only a fraction of a second. After only a second or so there would be another burst. The sequence was so regular that it varied by less than one part in ten million.

There was no explanation for the pulses. It was suggested that maybe they were signals generated by some far-off civilization that was trying to get in touch with other parts of the universe. For want of a better name, the sources of the pulses were referred to as LGM's —Little Green Men. Newspapers caused quite a flurry when they announced a strong possibility that there were other civilizations out there somewhere beaming radio signals to us.

It is questionable if any astronomers ever accepted the idea that the pulses were "man-made." If any did, they changed their minds as the pulses were studied. In order for the signals to reach us, immensely powerful generators would be required. Also, the pulses were spread across the various wavelengths of radio waves; a "man-generated" signal would be focused to a certain frequency, just as are radio and television broadcasts here on the earth. The pulses seemed to be produced naturally, and so "LGM" was dropped and instead the phenomena were called pulsars, for pulsating stars. As additional pulsars were found (more than fifty have been located), they came to be identified by initial letters, for the observatory that found them: CP for Cambridge Pulsar, HP for Harvard Pulsar, NP for National Radio

Astronomy Observatory Pulsar, and simply PSR. The letters are followed by four numbers, which gave the right ascension in hours and minutes—for example, CP0328, HP1506, PSR1749. Pulsar CP0328 is located at 3 hours 28 minutes ($3^h 28^m$ or $03^h 28^m$) right ascension. (Right ascension is an angular measurement made eastward along the celestial equator. To get a precise location, the declination—distance north or south of the celestial equator—is also needed. This is provided in tabulations of pulsars. The two figures, right ascension and declination, give the location of the star, much as latitude and longitude give the location of places on the Earth.)

Once the pulses were received, astronomers studied them to learn more about the sources producing them. What could they be like? The pulses were separated by intervals of just over a second. This meant the sources had to be very small, because a body gives off pulses whose lengths are determined by the time required for light to travel across it. For example, suppose the Sun were turned off all of a sudden. First we would see a dark spot at the center, because that's the location on the surface that is closest to us. The spot would grow larger rapidly until there was a black disk surrounded by a ring of light. Then it too would be extinguished. The time required for the dark spot to grow and reach the edge of the Sun would be about 2 seconds. If the Sun were to flash on and off (behave like a pulsar), the period could not be any less than 2 seconds. The periods of pulsars were measured as small fractions of seconds, so the pulsars had to be much smaller—only about 15 kilometers across.

Were they nearby, or at great distances? A clue to the answer was in the nature of the pulses: they were composed of long and short radio waves mixed together. If the waves were moving through a perfect vacuum, they would all travel at the same speed. But they were

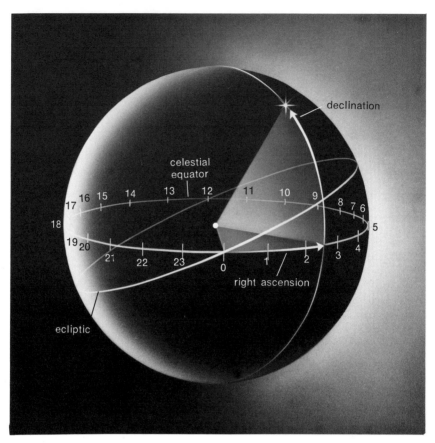

Right ascension, measurement eastward from the vernal equinox, and declination, measurement north or south of the celestial equator, give the locations of sky objects.

traveling through ionized gases (gases made of atoms that had lost electrons). The gases were very nebulous—estimated at only one electron in 10 cubic centimeters—nevertheless they existed. This meant the short wavelengths arrived at the Earth shortly before the longer wavelengths; the longer wavelengths were slowed down by the ions. By measuring this interval carefully, astronomers found that CP1919, the first pulsar to be discovered, is about 425 light years away. It is well within our own galaxy—rather close by actually, when one considers that the diameter of the galaxy is some 100,000 light years.

One year later, in 1968, astronomers turned once more to the Crab Nebula. Pulsars seem to be very small, very dense objects that release tremendous amounts of energy. They are precisely the kind of object that should be at the center of a nebula. Scannings of the area were

Signals received from the star indicated by the arrow reveal that it is a pulsar. The chart at the upper right shows regions of equal radio intensity. The graph shows changes in intensity of the radio waves. (Hale Observatories)

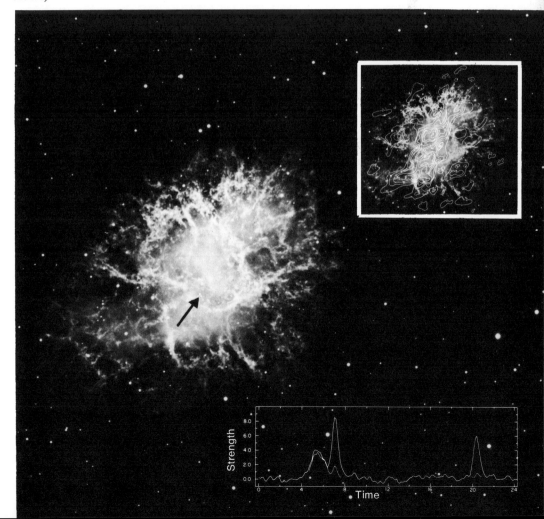

successful—a pulsar (NP0532) was found. This central star had been studied for decades, but no one knew it was a pulsar, although some had thought it probably was. All that was needed to prove it was a pulsar was equipment that could measure the pulses it was giving off —pulses that occur thirty times a second.

As do all pulsars, this star ejects particles from its surface, and these particles are accelerated in a powerful magnetic field. When the pulsar was as large as the Sun or larger, it had a magnetic field. When it became a pulsar, that field, which had covered the entire star (more than a million kilometers across), was concentrated into an area only a few kilometers across. The strength of the magnetic field became colossal—hundreds of billions of times greater than that of the Earth. You might even think of the star as a powerful rotating magnet, one that is spinning around some thirty times a second. Since it was discovered, the pulsar's period of rotation has lengthened. NP0532 is slowing down—not very much, but enough to tell us that after 10 million years (a very short time in terms of star lifetimes) it will no longer produce energy. It will be identifiable only by its gravitation.

Scientists believe they understand what will eventually happen to these incredible stars, and they have some idea of how their energy is generated. But they still do not know why the energy is pulsed. Consider the Sun for a moment: it is a star that is steadily radiating energy that arrives at the Earth as an even flow. Even though the Sun is rotating, the energy we receive from it is steady. Century after century it has remained essentially the same, so all parts of the Sun must be radiating fairly equal amounts of energy. But energy from neutron stars arrives in pulses. Theories to explain this have been proposed.

One theory is called the "lighthouse" idea. Perhaps the radio waves (also light and X rays) from NP0532, the pulsar in the Crab, are generated in only a small, localized region of the star and not over the entire surface. The waves radiate from that region in a cone shape, somewhat like a beam of light from a lighthouse. The neutron star is rotating very rapidly, some thirty times in one second. As it turns, the cone sweeps through space. Since it happens to pass over the Earth—that is, since the active region lines up with us—we receive the signal, the interval between pulses being determined by the rotation period of the star. If this theory is correct, we would receive pulses only from those stars rotating at an angle that causes the cone to sweep over the Earth. Conceivably, there could be several neutron stars at the center of the Crab, for example, each of which is producing energy. But since the cones of most of them do not pass over the Earth, we would not be aware of their presence. The lighthouse idea is supported by many astronomers.

Another theory has been built around the tremendous magnetic field of a pulsar. Electrons given off by the pulsar are held in the magnetic field. They form an "atmosphere" extending great distances beyond the star surface. As the pulsar spins, the ionized atmosphere is pulled around by the magnetic field. The rapid rotation would cause the outer edge of the atmosphere to move very fast—very close to the speed of light. Eventually the particles at the outer edge break away. As they do, radio waves are generated and the waves form into a beam, it is believed.

While each of these ideas has merit, astronomers are a long way from fully understanding either of them. The answer to the pulsations may lie in them—or, as has been suggested, pulsars may actually be two stars in orbit around a central point. Interactions between the stars may produce the pulsations. On the other hand, the phenome-

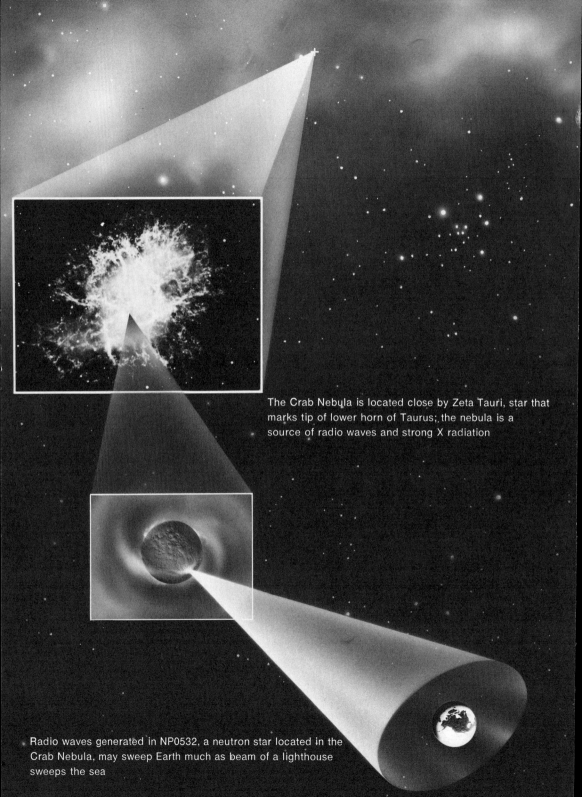

The Crab Nebula is located close by Zeta Tauri, star that marks tip of lower horn of Taurus; the nebula is a source of radio waves and strong X radiation

Radio waves generated in NP0532, a neutron star located in the Crab Nebula, may sweep Earth much as beam of a lighthouse sweeps the sea non may result from entirely different and completely unknown circumstances.

The fate of a neutron star is determined. After billions of years (longer than the age of our galaxy) the neutron star will become a cold, immensely dense mass of matter. It will produce no radio waves, no light, no radiation of any kind. The only clue to its presence will be its gravitation.

Not all stars will become neutron stars. It is believed that should a star have a mass close to 1.25 times that of the Sun (the critical mass), it will be able to withstand gravitational collapse. The collapse will cease when the neutron-star stage is reached. Should the mass of the original star be at least 2 times greater than the mass of the Sun, it is believed that gravitational collapse will continue. The once bright, radiating star will become a black hole—a mass so called because it cannot be observed by light-gathering telescopes, radio telescopes, or in any other way. Its tremendous gravitation keeps all kinds of radiation from escaping.

(Hale Observatories)

BLACK HOLES

No one has ever seen a black hole. In fact no one ever could, for no light escapes from them, no radio waves, X rays, or gamma rays. However, today's astronomers believe they exist. And the belief is not a new one, for discovery of the presence of black holes was predicted in the 1930s by several scientists, including J. Robert Oppenheimer, Walter Baade, and Fritz Zwicky. In fact the story begins even earlier. In 1798 the French astronomer Pierre Simon de Laplace theorized that if a body were massive enough and concentrated enough it would be invisible. He said escape velocity at its surface would be greater than the speed of light.

Escape velocity is the velocity something needs to escape from a given mass. For example, escape velocity from the surface of the Earth is 11 kilometers a second; a lunar vehicle must reach that velocity in order to enter an orbit that will intercept the Moon. Light travels some 300 000 kilometers a second, so it escapes from the Earth easily. The Sun has a much greater mass than the Earth, so the gravitation of the Sun is greater and therefore escape velocity is higher. Still, the speed of light is so high it escapes the Sun easily. (Because of the Sun's gravity there is a slight slow-down of the light, but not enough to change it.)

On a neutron star the situation is different. The gravitation of a neutron star is incredibly high. Light can escape from it, but because of the strong gravitation some energy is removed. As a result the light is reddened; red light is less energetic than blue light.

As mass, density, and gravitation increase, the light falls back more and more, just as a ball thrown upward comes down. Escape velocity from a black hole is greater than 3×10^5 kilometers per second (the speed of light); therefore no light can escape. Thus the name "black hole." Let's consider the size of these holes—which result, someone has said, when matter digs a hole, jumps in, and then pulls the hole in after it. You recall that the Sun is about 1 400 000 kilometers in diameter. If the mass of the Sun were compressed to one hundredth of its size, the star would be a white dwarf—one some 14 000 kilometers in diameter. White dwarfs that collapse still further become neutron stars. Such a star may be only 14 kilometers in diameter. Yet it contains the matter that was in the original star. This is the stopping place for those stars having a mass about equal to that of the Sun.

More massive stars collapse still further: they become black holes. When the mass has a diameter of only about 5 kilometers, gravitation has become strong enough to prevent the escape of all radiation. But the contraction does not stop. Theory says that contraction will continue—the mass will get smaller and smaller because there is no force powerful enough to stop the collapse. Density is already so high (trillions and trillions of tons of matter are packed into the small sphere) that a cubic centimeter would weigh a billion tons or more. But the mass gets smaller. The body may become no larger than a basketball —then contract to the size of a grain of sand—of an atom. And this small volume contains the mass of the original star.

How can this be?

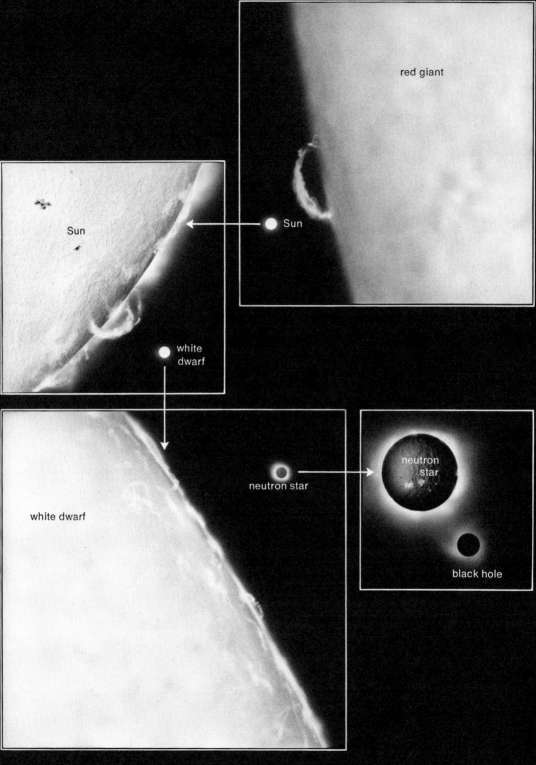

We know that matter cannot be packed so tightly. We know that matter must occupy space. But here we have just the opposite happening: more and more matter occupying less and less space. Apparently the ordinary laws of science do not apply here, nor do the special laws that were discovered by Albert Einstein. As scientists learn more about these black holes, new laws of science may be discovered, laws that will permit explanations of the events believed to occur.

These events happen in seconds. Once the mass is packed so tightly that there are billions of tons in one cubic centimeter, neutrons are squeezed into even smaller particles, called hyperons. The collapse continues until the *volume becomes zero and the density reaches infinity*. An instant before this happens, the collapsing mass gives off X rays. Surrounding the central mass are plasma clouds. Plasma is made of atoms that have been stripped of electrons; a plasma cloud is an electrified field of subatomic particles.

Toward the end of that second, even X rays cannot escape. The star disappears. A dim halo may remain where the final X rays react with the plasma to produce light, and the X rays themselves become visible light.

Writing in *Scientific American,* Kip Thorne, an astronomer at the

A red giant may have about the same mass as the Sun—that is, it may contain the same amount of material. But its diameter of 325 million kilometers would be some 250 times greater than the diameter of the Sun.

The diameter of the Sun (1 390 000 kilometers) is 100 times greater than the diameter of a white dwarf. Their masses are the same.

The diameter of a white dwarf (about that of the Earth) is some 700 times greater than the diameter of a neutron star; masses are the same.

A neutron star—14 kilometers in diameter—becomes a black hole when it collapses to a diameter of less than 5 kilometers. The mass of the black hole is the same as that of the Sun.

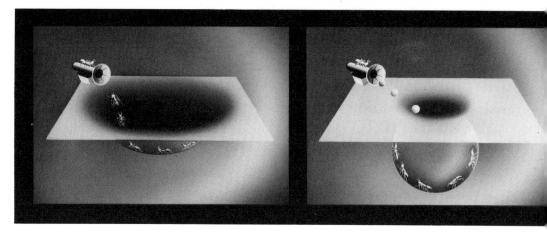

A parable: the journey of the ants into a black hole. The membrane supporting the ants contracted and collapsed (left).

Signal balls were sent to the one remaining ant. Traveling at the speed of light, they were sent at regular intervals but were received further and further apart (right).

California Institute of Technology, illustrated gravitational collapse with a fable about six ants. Once upon a time, he said, six ants lived on a large, thin rubber membrane. These ants communicated with one another by signal balls that rolled along the membrane at the speed of light.

One day five of the ants happened to gather near the center of the membrane. Their weight caused the membrane to bend; it started to collapse. The sixth ant was far away from the others with a special instrument for receiving the signal balls.

Being curious, the five ants decided not to try to escape. Instead, they would follow the downward collapse of the membrane. As the collapse continued, one of the ants decided to send signal balls to ant Number 6. Perhaps he would be able to tell Number 6 what was happening.

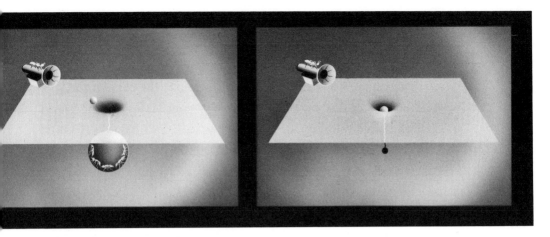

The last ball to leave the hole was received only after a very long time (left).

The next signal ball never escaped because the rate of collapse had become equal to the speed of light. (right).

There were two motions of the membrane. The surface contracted toward the center, and as a result everything on the membrane moved closer to the center. Also, the membrane bent into a sharp curve that would eventually collapse everything to infinite density.

As the collapse proceeded, the membrane contracted faster and faster. As a result the signal balls, which were sent in the direction opposite that of the contraction and at equally spaced intervals—say, a fraction of a second apart—were received by ant Number 6 at more and more widely spaced intervals, each a little longer than the preceding one.

An instant before the ant sending the signals reached the edge of the hole, it sent out ball Number 14.999. Because this ball was going slightly faster than the speed of collapse, it reached ant Number 6— but only after a long time.

Ball Number 15 was sent out 15 minutes after the collapse started, just as the ant sending it entered the region of no escape. The ball never reached ant Number 6. It stayed forever at the edge of the hole because at that point the membrane was contracting at the speed of light, the same speed as the speed of the ball. Ball Number 15.001, and every ball after that, never escaped from the hole.

The five ants inside the area experienced a fast collapse to infinite density. But ant Number 6, who was outside, unable to look into the hole, and who got all his information from the signal balls, believed that the collapse never went beyond the development of the hole, since after ball Number 14.999 he received no further information.

So it is with collapsed stars—just before the "hole" is reached we pick up X rays from the area around its edge.

It is believed that much greater masses than single massive stars may collapse into black holes. Perhaps millions or even billions of stars have collapsed into mammoth black holes at the centers of galaxies. If they did, tremendous amounts of energy would be generated. Some investigators suggest that explosions that have been observed at the centers of distant galaxies may have been caused by such collapses. Others propose that quasars are black holes in reverse.

Quasars produce energy (much of it in the form of visible light) in tremendous amounts—amounts comparable to that produced by an entire galaxy. Yet quasars are believed to be very small, not much greater in size than a single massive star. There are stages beyond black holes, some say, when the fantastic amounts of material in a massive black hole undergo changes that result in their release and conversion into radiation of many kinds. A black hole becomes a white hole. Maybe a quasar is an explosive reappearance of a massive black hole.

Until the early 1970s there were no observations to justify the theo-

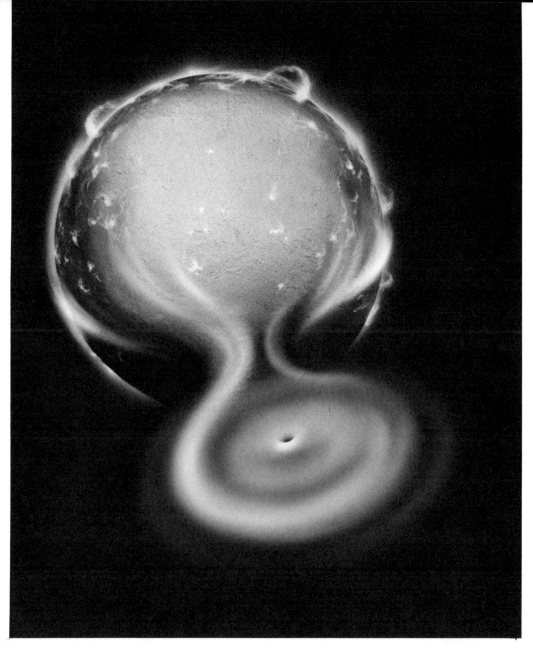

A black hole may be a member of a two-star system. High-energy X rays may be given off as gases from the companion star are pulled into the hole.

The region of the constellation Cygnus contains many complex star systems producing strong radiation in light, radio, and X-ray wavelengths.

retical ideas mentioned above. Black holes had never been seen. There was no way to detect them because they released no X rays, no light, no radio waves. The only clue to their presence was gravitation.

The gravitational force of a black hole, it was reasoned, is so strong that even at a considerable distance the force would be great enough to trap and hold a star. The black hole could be an unseen member of a two-star system, two masses going around one another. Also because of the strong gravitation, material from the companion star would be pulled away. As these gases entered the black hole their velocity would be so high that they would heat sufficiently to give off X rays. Because the black hole would be rotating very rapidly (several hundred times a second), and because the two "stars" would be revolving rapidly, the gases would not sink directly into the black hole; they would first form a disk around it. As they were pulled in, the temperature and pressure would produce X rays thousands of times more energetic than those emitted by the Sun.

Because X rays cannot penetrate our atmosphere, instruments to detect them must be carried outside it. Identification of sources had been difficult because the flights of the balloons and rockets used were short and the equipment was in early stages of development. In 1970 a small Earth-circling satellite called Uhuru, equipped with sophisticated X-ray detectors, was put into orbit. This satellite and others, including one called Copernicus, identified over one hundred sources of X radiation. Several of these sources were located in the region of Cygnus, the Swan, a constellation that appears in the summer skies of the Northern Hemisphere. The location of the first source discovered was found to coincide with a binary star, Cygnus X-1, one member of which is invisible. The partner star can be identified by slight perturbations it produces in the motion of the visible star. Also, periodic variations in the light of the visible star may result from regular movement of the invisible star in front of and then in back of it.

Careful investigation revealed that Cygnus X-1 is a supergiant star that is revolving around something once every 5.6 days. Astronomers determined that the mass of the unseen object is eight times that of the Sun. This is much too massive to be a white dwarf, or even a neutron star. The brightness of the supergiant varies twice during the 5.6-day cycle. If the supergiant is deformed by the attraction of the invisible object into an elongated formation of bright gases, brightness would be greatest at those times when the entire surface of the elongation is across our line of sight, that is, twice during each revolution.

Many believe that Cygnus X-1 is a supergiant star and a black hole. Cygnus X-3 is believed to be a similar system. Careful observation of the Cygnus objects has revealed that they behave erratically as well. Every once in a while there are flare-ups; intensity becomes much greater. Proponents of the black-hole explanation say that the flare-ups occur in the plasma cloud surrounding the nucleus. This is probably true, although complete and acceptable explanations of these flare-ups have not been presented. Perhaps they are due to a condition of black holes that has not yet been considered. Some investigators think that the flare-ups argue against the existence of black holes. They believe that in Cygnus X-1 we are "seeing" phenomena that do not fit into the black-hole definition. Perhaps so—but astronomers who have spent considerable time working out the theory of black holes are quite convinced that explanations of all the observations will be forthcoming and that they will reveal we are indeed "seeing" black holes.

Black holes—fantastically small concentrations of stupendous

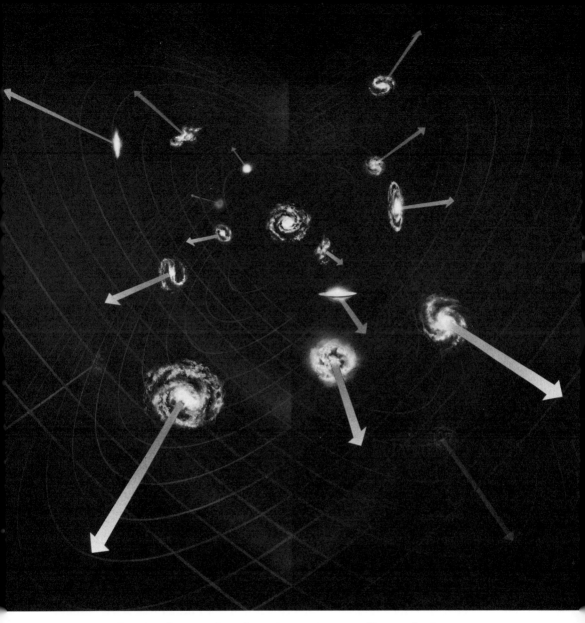

Present evidence indicates that the universe is expanding; galaxies are receding from us in all directions. Those farthest away move at the greatest velocity. Eventually the process may be reversed—the universe may collapse.

amounts of matter—may hold the answer to one of the really perplexing mysteries of the universe: what has happened to the matter of which it is composed?

It is believed that the matter in the galaxies (the entire universe) was at one time tightly packed together into a "Super Atom" that exploded in a "Big Bang." In the process, stars were formed, clusters of stars, galaxies, and clusters of galaxies. Since that cataclysmic moment the galaxies have been moving away from one another; the universe has been expanding. Unless there is something to stop it, a movement, once started, continues forever. Observations imply that the velocity of the galaxies is decreasing—the expansion of the universe is slowing down. If it really is, then the mass of the universe must be sufficient to exert enough gravitation to hold it together.

But there is a discrepancy. When all the observed matter (and all the matter we can assume exists) is added up, the total turns out to be much less than that needed to prevent everlasting expansion. The black dwarfs (cinders of neutron stars) and black holes of the universe may contain enough mass to provide a major part of the difference. Eventually, contraction of the universe may cause our galaxy and the billions of other galaxies to pack together into a Super Black Hole—perhaps much like the Super Atom from which it all began.

Black holes, and the other stars we've been considering, come about because of gravitation. Contraction produces heat, which initiates nuclear reactions. These reactions continue until the "fuel" is consumed; then gravitation takes over. Matter is compressed into dwarf stars, into neutron stars, and ultimately into black holes where volume is zero and density is infinite. Then, all matter of the universe is pulled into a Super Atom, which, we expect, will thereupon explode. According to this viewpoint, the universe is ongoing, everlasting, living through cycles of billions of years of expanding, contracting, exploding.

Or our universe may not be everlasting. Black holes may be the sinks of the universe, as some have suggested. Matter may disappear into them—but it may reappear explosively, not in our universe, but in a universe quite different from the one we know.

Such ideas are fantastic, but they are at the threshold of thinking in this last quarter of the twentieth century.

Appendixes

THE MAGNITUDE SCALE

The brightness of stars and other objects is given as their magnitude. The magnitude scale of brightness had its beginning centuries ago. Ptolemy, the Egyptian astronomer, gave the approximate magnitude (importance) of stars in his catalogue, which appeared in the second century. The brightest stars, the most important, were called first-magnitude stars. Dimmer stars were of the second magnitude, and so on to sixth magnitude—the dimmest stars that could be identified.

When instruments to measure light became available, it was possible to determine differences in brightness exactly, rather than estimating them as Ptolemy had done. It was found that the degree of difference between successive magnitudes amounted to a value of 2.512. A first-magnitude star is about 2.5 times dimmer than a 0-magnitude star; a second-magnitude star is about 6.3 (2.512 $\times$ 2.512) times dimmer; and so on.

STAR MAGNITUDE	RATIO OF BRIGHTNESS
1	2.5:1
2	6.3:1
3	16:1
4	40:1
5	100:1
10	10,000:1

In some of the tables below, magnitude values are given. Those objects having the highest magnitudes are the dimmest; those with smaller numbers are brighter. In some cases the object is so bright it has a negative magnitude. Such objects are much brighter than the brightest stars.

Here are some comparative magnitudes:

Sun	—26.8
Full Moon	—12.0
Venus at brightest	—4.0
Sirius	—1.4
Rigel	+0.1
Polaris	+2.0
Limit of unaided vision	+6.0
Limit of 200-inch telescope	+23.5

SPECTRUM CLASSIFICATION

One way of classifying stars is by the light spectra they produce. These are then put in order, from the very hottest stars to the coolest, and categorized by letter designations.

Initially, A type stars were thought to be the hottest (the most luminous) stars; B type stars the second in order; and so on. Improved measuring techniques and greater knowledge resulted in a rearrangement of classes—thus the departure from alphabetical order. Examples of each spectral type, including range in temperature and some of the principal materials found, are given below.

TYPE	NAME OF STAR	TEMPERATURE RANGE (°K)		MORE ABUNDANT MATERIAL(S)	COLOR
O	Naos	30 000 to	60 000	Helium	Blue-white
B	Spica	12 000 to	25 000	Helium	Blue-white
A	Vega	8 000 to	11 000	Hydrogen	White
F	Procyon	6 200 to	7 200	Hydrogen, metals	Yellow-white
G	Sun	4 600 to	6 000	Hydrogen, metals	Yellow
K	Arcturus	3 500 to	4 900	Calcium	Orange
M	Antares	2 600 to	3 500	Titanium	Orange-red
R	Variables	2 000 to	3 000	Zirconium	Red
N	Alpha Cygni	2 000 to	3 000	Carbon	Deep red

THE 25 BRIGHTEST STARS

NAME	CONSTELLATION	APPARENT MAGNITUDE
Sun	—	—26.80
Sirius	Canis Major	—1.43
Canopus	Carina	—0.73
Alpha Centauri	Centaurus	—0.27
Arcturus	Boötes	—0.06
Vega	Lyra	0.04
Capella	Auriga	0.09
Rigel	Orion	0.15
Procyon	Canis Minor	0.37
Achernar	Eridanus	0.53
Beta Centauri	Centaurus	0.66
Betelgeuse	Orion	0.70
Altair	Aquila	0.80
Aldebaran	Taurus	0.85
Alpha Crucis	Crux	0.87
Antares	Scorpius	0.98
Spica	Virgo	1.00
Fomalhaut	Piscis Austrinus	1.16
Pollux	Gemini	1.16
Deneb	Cygnus	1.26
Beta Crucis	Crux	1.31
Regulus	Leo	1.36
Adhara	Canis Major	1.49
Castor	Gemini	1.59
Shaula	Scorpio	1.62

THE 15 NEAREST STARS

NAME	DISTANCE (LIGHT YEARS)	APPARENT MAGNITUDE	SPECTRAL TYPE
Sun	—	—26.8	G
Alpha Centauri	4.3	0.3	G
Barnard's Star*	5.9	9.5	M
Wolf 359	7.6	13.5	M
Lalande 21185	8.1	7.5	M
Sirius	8.6	—1.4	A
Luyten	8.9	12.5	M
Ross 154	9.4	10.6	M
Ross 248	10.3	12.2	M
Epsilon Eridani	10.7	3.7	K
Luyten 789–6	10.8	12.2	M
Ross 128	10.8	11.1	M
61 Cygni	11.2	5.2	K
Epsilon Indi	11.2	4.7	K
Procyon	11.4	0.3	F

* Barnard's Star shows a large proper motion. This means it moves quite a bit compared with the motions of nearby stars. Most stars move along a straight line. However, some observers believe they detect a side-to-side motion as Barnard's Star travels forward. These same observers have computed that the wobble could be explained by supposing there are two large masses moving around the star and pulling it from side to side. These masses, if they do exist, would be of the proper size to be called planets.

Most stars are too far away for us to be able to observe slight side-to-side motions. However, many astronomers believe that they probably do move in this way, as a result of the presence of planet-size masses. Probably millions of stars have planets moving around them.

Suggested Further Reading

Aitken, R. C., *The Binary Stars*. N.Y.: Dover, 1964.

Branley, Franklyn M., *The Sun: Star Number One*. N.Y.: Crowell, 1964.

————, and Mark R. Chartrand, *Astronomy*. N.Y.: Crowell, 1975.

Page, T., and L. W. Page, eds., *The Evolution of Stars*. N.Y.: Macmillan, 1968.

Pickering, James Sayre, *The Stars Are Yours* (rev. ed.). N.Y.: Macmillan, 1958.

Tayler, R. J., *The Stars: Their Structure and Evolution*. N.Y.: Wykeham, 1970.

Bok, Bart J., "The Birth of a Star." *Scientific American*, August 1972.

Burbidge, Geoffrey, "Dissecting the Crab." *Natural History*, October 1970.

Eben, Icko, Jr., "Globular Star Clusters." *Scientific American*, July 1970.

Hewish, Antony, "Pulsars." *Scientific American*, October 1968.

Thorne, Kip S., "Gravitational Collapse." *Scientific American*, November 1967.

Weaver, Kenneth F., "The Incredible Universe." *National Geographic*, May 1974.

Index

ABOUT THE AUTHOR

Franklyn M. Branley, Astronomer Emeritus and former Chairman of The American Museum–Hayden Planetarium, is the author of many books, pamphlets, and articles on various aspects of science for young readers. BLACK HOLES, WHITE DWARFS, AND SUPERSTARS is the eighth in the Exploring Our Universe series, written by Dr. Branley and illustrated by Helmut Wimmer.

Dr. Branley holds degrees from New York University, Columbia University, and the State University of New York College at New Paltz. He and his wife live in Woodcliff Lake, New Jersey, and spend their summers at Sag Harbor, New York.

ABOUT THE ILLUSTRATOR

Helmut Wimmer was born in Munich, Germany, and was apprenticed at the age of fourteen as a sculptor and architectural model-maker. After World War II he worked as a sculptor in the restoration of damaged buildings in Russia, where he had been a prisoner of war, and also in Germany. In 1954 Mr. Wimmer came to the United States and began a new career as a painter of astronomical subjects and Art Supervisor of The American Museum–Hayden Planetarium. His paintings have been exhibited in many cities around the United States and have also appeared in *Graphis, Physics Today, Smithsonian Magazine, Natural History,* and many other magazines. With his wife and children, he lives in Bergenfield, New Jersey.